FINANCIAL SECTOR OF THE AMERICAN ECONOMY

edited by

STUART BRUCHEY
UNIVERSITY OF MAINE

A GARLAND SERIES

BANKING GEOGRAPHY OF THE UNITED STATES

STRUCTURE, CONDUCT, AND PERFORMANCE
OF COMMERCIAL BANKS IN THE
U.S. METROPOLITAN SYSTEM

BIN ZHOU

GARLAND PUBLISHING, INC.
NEW YORK & LONDON / 1997

Library of Congress Cataloging-in-Publication Data

Zhou, Bin, 1956–
 Banking geography of the United States : structure, conduct,
and performance of commercial banks in the U.S. metropolitan
system / Bin Zhou.
  p.   cm. — (Financial sector of the American economy)
 Revision of the author's thesis (Ph. D.)—Univ. of Georgia,
1994.
 Includes bibliographical references and index.
 ISBN 0-8153-2794-3 (alk. paper)
 1. Banks and banking—United States. 2. Banks and banking—Mathematical models. I. Title. II. Series.
HG2491.Z48 1997
332.1'0973—dc21
                                                    96-48391

Printed on acid-free, 250-year-life paper
Manufactured in the United States of America

This book is dedicated to my family: my late father Zhou Zhaohu, my mother Peng Juexun, my sisters Zhou Xuan and Zhou Ping, and my wife Wendy Shaw. Their love for me made possible the completion of this work.

Contents

Tables

Illustrations

Acknowledgements

I would like to thank Dr. James O. Wheeler, Dr. Susan Davies-Withers, Dr. Hugh O. Nourse, Dr. Clifton W. Pannell, Dr. Kavita K. Pandit of the University of Georgia, Dr. Jean-Claude Thill of the University of New York at Buffalo, and Dr. Ronald M. Mitchelson of Morehead State University, Kentucky, for their contribution and guidance during the production of this banking study. Special thanks go to my wife Wendy Shaw for her unfailing patience and support.

Banking Geography of the United States

I

Introduction

BACKGROUND

The financial industry in general, and the banking industry in particular, is an extremely important part of the U.S. economy. The role played by the financial industry in the economy can be depicted by the following macroeconomic identity:

$$C + I + G + X = Y = C + S + T + M$$

Here C is the amount of consumption; I investment; G government expenditures; X exports; Y gross national product; S savings; T taxes; and M imports. The left-hand side of the model indicates the composition of the total demand of society, that is, what the society plans to spend money on. The right-hand side indicates the composition of the total supply of society, that is, where the total income goes.

From the right-hand side, it is seen that part of the total income is injected into savings, which relies on savings absorption functions by various financial institutions. From the left-hand side, it is seen that the savings absorbed can be channeled to different uses: consumption, investment, and government spending, which are realized by various financial institutions: commercial loans, mortgage lending, and securities issuance.

A part of the above function is carried out by the commercial banks. As financial intermediaries, the basic functions of commercial banks are to pool funds from individuals and institutions at large and to make funds available to various private and public sectors. All these activities are carried out in a spatial context. Here "the spatial context" contains both internal and external aspects. Internally, a banking firm may be a spatial entity. That is, a commercial bank may have operating units in a number of locations, forming an operating network. The overall production processes constitute sub-components that are spatially separate. As a special case, the network of a unit bank shrinks to a point in space. Thus, a banking firm is not only an institutional framework for resource allocation, but also an operational entity where the resource allocation occurs in a spatial context.

Externally, banks deal with their markets and customers. Market information and customers are always place specific. Although different banking firms may have the same number of branches, they may spread their networks into different metropolitan markets. Thus, different firms may obtain market information and customers from quite different areas. Such variation in external environments will necessarily affect the decision-making process of banking firms, thus affecting the spatial behavior and performance of a firm.

Given the geographic context of banking operations, questions arise as to how to conceptualize the resource allocation process in a spatial context. What are the spatial and hierarchical patterns of the place banking network? How do different banking networks affect banking performance? These questions present several logically related and cohesive issues concerning various aspects of the geography of banking. A conceptual understanding of banking resource allocation in a spatial context would provide insight into the explanation of banking conduct and operational mechanisms. Such banking conduct and operational mechanisms, in turn, help shape the aggregate place hierarchical networks in banking. These banking locational networks may also affect banking performance.

An understanding of these issues has important theoretical and empirical significance. For a long time, location theory has been the backbone of theoretical economic geography. The classical industrial and agricultural location theories address the issue of firm resource allocation in a spatial context. The firms are assumed to use the fixed inputs (the Leontief technology) and produce a given level of output. Using theory of production as the major conceptual framework, neoclassical location theorists have extended classical location problems into generalized Weber and von Thünen problems. Generalized location theory assumes that firms use substitutable input technology and that the optimal level of output, optimal combination of inputs, and optimal firm location are determined simultaneously. However, much of the location study based on the neoclassical theory of production has addressed the issue of firm location in which the firm has only one operating unit. The neoclassical theory of production has not been extended into a multi-unit firm resource allocation problem. Against the contemporary business environment where multi-unit firms are dominant, such inadequate effort by neoclassical location theorists constitutes a distinct theoretical gap in describing micro-level resource allocation. Such inadequacy is especially evident in the study of banking geography since most major banks are multi-unit in nature.

In recent years, the study of corporate geography has rapidly risen to prominence in the field of urban, economic geography. As an extremely promising subject for theoretical and empirical investigation, corporate geography addresses the location issues of decision-making units and associated producer services. While theoretical study of locational issues concerning corporate headquarters is still at the preliminary, inductive stage, the empirical study of corporate command/control networks has generated a rich literature. Since the banking industry plays an important role in corporate financing and metropolitan economies, the study of the geography of banking has become an important component of corporate geography. Although the empirical investigation of the banking command and control landscape, and the spatial concentration of banking assets have received much attention, concrete geographic networks of banking command and control, and spatial concentrations of banking ownership have never been systematically revealed. In most studies, the size of banking assets controlled by a place has been used as an indication of degree of prominence and status in a banking command and control hierarchy. The banking ties between places are largely derived from differences in size, rather than from a detailed investigation of banking ownership. Results from a study of this nature can only provide an approximation of the actual geographic distribution of banking command/control function.

The multi-locational nature of many banking firms naturally leads to the question of how a multi-location bank performs differently, compared with a unitary bank. This issue is closely related to U.S banking structure and especially banking deregulation since the early 1980s. The contemporary banking structure of the United States was established during the banking reform precipitated by the Great Depression. The McFadden Act of 1927, the Glass-Steagle Act of 1933, and the Bank Holding Company Act of 1965, as amended in 1970, put product and geographic restrictions on banking. Rising interest rates and competition from other financial and nonfinancial institutions since the 1960s and during the 1970s precipitated banking deregulation beginning in the early 1980s. Geographic restrictions on banking were also challenged on the grounds that by limiting geographic expansion, the benefits from economies of scale and geographic diversification were unduly prohibitive to banks. Although until the late 1980s and early 1990s, interstate banking through banking holding companies had been allowed in most states, there had been variations among states in the extent to which interstate banking was allowed. In addition, interstate branching was still disallowed in most states. The call for a more liberal banking environment has intensified since. The Treasure Plan of 1987 called for eliminating all restrictions on branching across state boundaries. Interstate banking and interstate branching legislation has become an important topic in congressional debates since the 1980s. In 1994, the Riegle-Neal Interstate Banking and Branching Efficiency Act was signed into law authorizing, for the first time in the U.S. history, nationwide interstate banking and branching.

Such debate over interstate banking and branching has partly hinged on the possible benefits obtained from multi-location banking, which in turn has precipitated empirical investigation of banking performance related to multi-location banking. Several problems emerged from this investigation. The first is the absence of spatial context. Many banking efficiency studies have focused on the investigation of economies of scale of banking operations. One underlying assumption in much of this research is that banking size is directly related to the number of branch banking offices. In other words, the space is replaced with firm sizes. This approach is less satisfactory in that it ignores the fact that different networks may exist in various external environments. The variations in banking performance that are related to differences in network locations may then be concealed. Furthermore, although some studies explicitly introduced the number of branches into their empirical investigation, the variations in network pattern have been ignored. In reality, some bank networks are concentrated in a single metropolitan area. Others spread their facilities over a certain number of metropolitan areas. Such variations in the geographic configuration of networks should also be accounted for. Most importantly, the heated debate over free branching across state boundaries has highlighted the fact that branching and banking holdings are generally seen as different mechanisms in achieving multiple location operations. Banking efficiency assessment should therefore distinguish between these different mechanisms in order to shed light on the issue of whether the interstate banking through branching can significantly improve banking performance as compared with interstate banking holding. To this day, investigation that focuses on such comparison has seldom been done.

RESEARCH QUESTIONS

This study intends to address the previously mentioned issues concerning banking spatial conduct, geographic network structure, and banking performance as affected by different network patterns. Specifically, this research addresses the following questions.

First, conceptually, how do we interpret micro- and macro-mechanisms of banking activity in a spatial context? That is, at the micro-level, what is the mechanism of resource allocation for a multi-input, multi-output, and multi-location banking firm? In addition, at the aggregate level, what is the mechanism that forms the economic ties between places? What is the economic foundation for the widely used spatial interaction model? These efforts constitute the first contribution of this study to location theory in general and to banking geography in particular.

Second, within the U.S metropolitan system, what is the aggregate banking place network structure? What is the geographic distribution of the banking ownership pattern under the branching network? How does bank holding change the geographic distribution of banking ownership patterns? What is the role of the largest metropolitan areas in the corporate banking landscape? Research on these issues will, for the first time, present a systematic study of metropolitan banking ownership landscape and constitutes the second contribution.

Third, in conjunction with the previous two sets of questions, does space make a difference in banking operation? That is, do banking firms with different spatial network patterns perform differently in terms of their operational efficiency? In light of different ownership, do branching operations differ from banking holding operations in terms of their banking efficiency? Would operational efficiency obtained from branching operations provide the foundation for free branching across state boundaries? Do banking networks located at different places have different banking efficiency?

In short, this study is concerned with issues in the banking industry about how firms make decisions concerning location, how places are connected, and how these connections affect firm performance. The first issue involves banking conduct at the firm level and at the industrial and community level. The second issue concerns the aggregate hierarchical place structure as a result of firm and industrial behavior. The third issue concerns consequences of individual firm conduct and aggregate industrial structure. Structure-conduct-performance (S-C-P) is an established approach in industrial organization analysis. However, a systematic analysis of the geographic aspects of S-C-P has been missing for the U.S. banking industry. Different issues are investigated within different fields. This study represents a preliminary effort in putting these issues under a consistent conceptual framework and addressing them in a systematical fashion.

METHODOLOGY AND DATA

This study adopts the production function as the major conceptual framework in analyzing micro- and macro-mechanisms of banking activity in a spatial context. The neoclassical theory of production is a useful analytical tool in analyzing firm behavior. This study adopts the conventional assumption of a profit maximization objective. The banking firm adjusts its resources among multiple inputs, multiple outputs, and multiple locations in order to achieve optimal resource allocation. To simplify the mathematical derivation, perfect competition is assumed.

With certain assumptions, the production function can also be used in analyzing aggregate production processes. This study uses a simple general equilibrium model where the utility function of one place and the production function of another interact to produce optimal banking asset holdings across space. Such a supply/demand relationship can then be conveniently translated into a generalized spatial interaction model. The spatial interaction model is then seen to be compatible with conventional production functions in a broad sense.

The notion of a production function is closely related to its dual: a cost function. A cost function is appropriate in conducting statistical estimation on firm performance when the firms are using multiple inputs and producing multiple outputs. The notion of economies of scale and scope can be readily estimated using a derived cost function. Recent developments in production/cost function analyses provide various options in terms of functional form. The conventional production function assumes separability and homogeneity. Such assumptions simplify the mathematical manipulation so some insight can be gained concerning production processes. However, in estimation practice, flexible forms of production/cost functions are preferred. A flexible function assumes no separability and homogeneity. With certain assumptions on values of certain parameters, this form can be easily translated into a homogeneous and separable function. Therefore, it has wide applicability.

The empirical study of the metropolitan banking ownership landscape requires network analysis. All metropolitan areas contained in the data sources are analyzed. This amounts to a 335-by-335 place matrix. An entry within the matrix is the magnitude of inter-place banking ownership, expressed by the amount of deposits and number of branches. Two types of ownership networks are investigated: networks under branching and networks under banking holding. Using a dominant-flow analysis approach, the banking networks are grouped into hierarchical systems and mapped. The typology of various hierarchical networks is identified using a designed approach. Major banking command and control centers are identified using a command/control index, C values.

Major sources of data for this study are magnetic computer tapes *Summary of Deposits for All FDIC-insured Depository Institutions* (the *Deposits tape*), and *Income Report Financial Statement For all Banks* (the *Income tape*). The metropolitan areas used are those defined in 1990, as reflected in *Bank Data Book, FDIC Insured Bank and Depositories, 1991*. The rank of metropolitan areas is based on 1990 metropolitan area population, as listed in the *State and Metropolitan Data Book, 1990*, supplemented by the *Census of the Population, 1990*. The *Deposits tape* contains deposit information for all commercial and saving banks and their branches. The location of bank headquarters and of each branch office, as well as their total withdrawable deposits are reported. From such information, place networks based on branch connections can be constructed. By coding banks and their offices within the *Deposits tape* with the bank holding company identification obtained from the *Income tape*, banks and their offices are grouped into bank holding companies. The place network under bank holding companies can then be constructed. The *Income tape* also contains important financial information such as total operating expenses, a breakdown of major cost groups, the amount of various deposits, the amounts of various loans, and the number of employees. These serve as a basis to estimate banking firm cost functions.

ORGANIZATION OF THE BOOK

Chapter II provides a brief history of the U.S. banking industry and addresses some important issues concerning the geographic dimensions of banking. Chapter III reviews the existing literature concerning banking production functions, banking firm performance assessment, and the corporate banking landscape. Chapters IV to VI contain the major contributions of this study. Chapter IV is devoted to a theoretical derivation of a micro-level banking firm production function and a macro-level general equilibrium spatial banking model. Chapter V presents a systematic analysis of place networks based on corporate banking ownership. Chapter VI discusses statistical estimation of banking efficiency. Chapter VII summarizes the findings and concludes the book.

II

A Brief History of the U.S.
Banking Industry

This chapter presents a brief history of the development of the U.S. banking industry and of related legislation, as a background for discussion of the issues proposed in the previous chapter. Emphasis is on the geographic dimensions of banking structure.

As Pierce (1991a) points out, the history of banking in the United States is a chronicle of struggles between bankers attempting to maximizing profits and government seeking to limit the power and instability of the banking industry. Intertwined have been conflicts between the federal government and states over the regulatory control of the banking industry. The current banking structure and, to a large extent, the banking crisis since the 1980s, are the legacy of these struggles and conflicts.

EARLY BANKING INDUSTRY

During the colonial period there were no banking institutions. Bank-like lending was mainly carried out by merchants. The staple precious metal went to London and Bristol via trade. Public financing through issuing bills of credit was also largely banned by the British. United States banking history began in 1782 when the Bank of North America was established in Philadelphia. The earliest banks were all state chartered and supervised. Between 1791 to 1811, and 1816 to 1836, the First and Second Banks of the United States were chartered by Congress functioning essentially as central banks. The monopolistic charter, extensive geographic networks, and substantial size generated fear and hostility toward large and centralized financial power from various local and federal interest groups. The Banks' charters were not renewed after running out. From 1837 to 1863, the Free Banking

11

Movement spread to many states. Chartering a bank no longer required special legislation but only the meeting of certain criteria. This speeded up the growth of state banks. In 1863, the National Banking Act established the Office of the Comptroller of the Currency to charter national banks in order to establish uniform currency and carry federal borrowing during war time. The United States had begun its dual banking system. The bank panic between 1893 and 1907 precipitated the need for a central bank providing liquidity in the face of weakened public confidence. In 1914, the Federal Reserve (Fed) was established based on the Federal Reserve Act. This loosely centralized bank proved to be inadequate in providing liquidity and banking safety during the 1930s depression (Park 1992). The result was fundamental banking reform in the years that followed.

BANKING REFORMS: THE 1930s AND 1980s

The cornerstone of the 1930s bank reform was provision of a banking safety net to control risk. This was accomplished by the establishment of the Federal Deposit Insurance Corporation (FDIC) to insure banking deposits, and relaxing of the criteria for borrowing from the Federal Reserve (Pierce 1991). Deposit insurance eliminates the incentive for insured depositors to stage bank runs. Relaxing lending criteria injects higher liquidity into the banking industry when necessary. The latter task is carried out by a restructured, more centrally controlled Fed. Other important reforms included separation of commercial banking from investment banking, putting ceilings on the interest rates charged on time and saving deposits (Regulation Q), and geographic restrictions on banking (Golembe 1992; Kamerschen 1991).

The result of these banking reforms was the creation of a safe and highly protected banking industry. Banks operated on their protected product and geographic turf. Local monopoly provides high profitability. Most bank failures between 1940s to 1960s were due to bank fraud. Depositors were protected from loss through deposit insurance.

Since the early 1960s, there have been major changes in the nation's macroeconomic environment, particularly high inflation, rising and volatile interest rates, and declining economic growth. The increased gap between ongoing interest rates on loans and controlled interest rates on deposits invited competition from nonbank banks such as finance companies, mutual funds, mortgage pools, securities firms, and financial firms affiliated with corporate America such as Sears, JC Penney, General Electric, etc. These competitors are not subject to the geographic, product, and interest rate restrictions imposed on banks, but can provide bank-like services, such as credit cards, consumer financing, cash management, and commercial papers. The result was a massive exodus of deposits and business loans from banks, a process called disintermediation: Funds are transferred directly among corporate and individual customers. The share of the banking industry in the nation's financial assets and income has steadily dropped (Kaufman 1993). Banks responded to these problems by issuing bank repo, negotiable orders of withdrawal (NOW), negotiable certificates of deposit (NCD), and money market deposit accounts; and increasing overseas banking and lending to less developed countries (LDCs). In addition, banking problems led the many banking firms, especially major banking companies, to appeal the existing banking regulation. Federal and state banking regulators also reevaluated the regulatory effects on the banking industry. Many banking companies and bank regulators concluded that electronic technologies used in delivering financial services have made conventional restrictions on banking largely irrelevant (Hove 1994). Removal of these restrictions would allow equal competition between banking organizations and nonbank banks, and thus, help strengthen the banking industry.

Such a combination of factors led to the banking deregulation in the early 1980s. The Depository Institution Reform and Monetary Control Act of 1980 and Garn-St. Germain Act of 1982 legalized various new instruments, set the stage to phase out regulation Q, and allowed banks, and thrifts, to enter new product lines such as commercial real estate lending. However, economic recession in the early 1980s caused widespread business failure in oil production and related commercial real estate. This caused a record number of bank failures since the Great Depression (Crawford and Sihler 1991; White 1993). The bulk of those failed banks were from the Southwest, Mountain, and New England regions. A weak world economy caused many LDCs to fail to pay back their debt. This, in turn, weakened large U.S. banks that were active in overseas banking (Taylor 1990). Another blow to the banking industry as a whole was the crisis of leveraged buyout (LBO). The 1980s saw waves of corporate mergers and acquisitions through leverage buyout: corporations issued debt to buy back their stocks. The increased leverage level created a huge junk bond market (Worthington 1993). Much of the LBO was financed through bank loans. In the late 1980s the junk bond market collapsed, putting further stress on banks (Miller 1990; Taylor 1990; White 1993). These waves of stress on banks, especially the high rise in bank failures, are alarming signs of banking decline, a phenomenon widely characterized as a banking crisis (Crawford and Silher 1991). The legacy of the 1980s has produced a weakened and vulnerable U.S. banking system from, according to Corrigan (1992), a combination of rising asset quality problems, rapidly rising operating costs, competitively depressed margins and spreads, weakened capital positions, and underlying banking structure that was (and is) increasingly out of step with the reality of the marketplace.

LEGAL FRAMEWORKS FOR BANKING GEOGRAPHIC EXPANSION

The banking crisis during the 1980s was caused by the combined force of economic, regulatory, and managerial and personal mistakes. One line of banking regulatory provision has attracted special attention from many economists and especially economic geographers. This is the regulatory restrictions on the geographic expansion of banks. Many writers blame such geographic restrictions for contributing to the banking crisis. The arguments underlying such blame seem logical: if economic force requires a bank to expand geographically, any legal restrictions on such a move would necessarily put undue constraints on bank operation, resulting in poor banking performance.

In the United States, two major mechanisms exist for banks to conduct legitimate expansion geographically: branch banking and banking through bank holding companies (Golembe and Holland 1986). Branch banking involves the establishment of fully owned *de novo* branch offices in locations other than a bank's head office. The first branch banking systems were the First and Second Banks of the United States. Their branch networks extended to all major cities. Such extensive geographic networks partly contributed to their own short lives. After the First and Second Banks of the United States, not only interstate branching was banned in all states, but also branching within states was largely prohibited (Golembe and Holland 1986; Miller 1990a). The 1864 National Bank Act did not explicitly specify the branching status for national banks. The Comptroller's interpretation of the Act prohibited establishment of branch offices for national banks. Toward the end of 19th century and in the early 20th century, economic concentration in cities resulted in rapid urbanization. Banks felt the need to follow their customers in an ever expanding urban area. Branching had shown benefit to banking. By the early part of this century, 20 or so states allowed in-state branch banking, although some of them put certain limitations on the scheme of branching in terms of branch locations and the number of branch offices a bank could establish (Miller 1990a). The Office of the Comptroller also revised its position and began to approve branches. The McFadden Act of 1927 allowed the national banks[1] to branch within the city of their head office operation if state banks could do the same. In 1933, amendments to the Act permitted national banks to branch wherever state banks in the same state were allowed to branch. Although permitted to branch, the national banks effectively were prohibited from interstate branching since almost all states prohibited branching by out-of-state banks.[2] Table 2.1 illustrates a chronology of pertaining to geographic banking regulation in the United States.

Before the 1994 Interstate Banking and Branching legislation, 35 states plus Washington DC allowed statewide branching (Alabama, Alaska, Arizona, California, Connecticut, Delaware, Florida, Hawaii, Idaho, Indiana, Kansas, Louisiana, Maine, Maryland, Massachusetts, Michigan, Missouri, Nevada, New Hampshire, New Mexico, North Carolina, Ohio, Oregon, Pennsylvania, Rhode Island, South Carolina, South Dakota, Tennessee, Texas, Utah, Vermont, Virginia, Washington, West Virginia, and Wisconsin); 12 states permitted statewide branching through bank merger (Colorado,[3] Georgia, Illinois, Kentucky, Minnesota, Mississippi, Montana, Nebraska, New York, North Dakota, Oklahoma, and Wyoming); 8 states allowed limited *de novo* branching, which means that there were limitations on branching in terms of branch locations and/or the number of branches a bank was allowed to have (Arkansas,[4] Georgia, Illinois, Iowa, Kentucky, Minnesota, Nebraska, and Wyoming).[5] In addition, a few states had legislation in place that allowed interstate branching, including Maryland, North Carolina, New York, and Rhode Island.

The second geographical expansion mechanism involves the bank holding company. In the late 19th century, the incentive for banking at multiple locations helped the development of two types of multi-office banking organization: chain banking and group banking. The former

Table 2.1 Chronology of Legislation Pertaining to Geographic Banking Regulation

	Branch Banking	Bank Holding
Early 1800s	Interstate branching 1st Bank of U. S (1791-1811), 2nd Bank of U. S. (1816-1836)	Interstate bank holding
1836-late 1800s	Interstate banking prohibited	
Since 1927	In-state branching for state banks In-state branching allowed for national banks (the McFadden Act of 1927, the Glass-Steagall Act of 1935)	
1956		Interstate bank holding prohibited (The Douglas Amendment to the Bank Holding Company Act of 1956)
1975		Maine's legislation of national reciprocal interstate banking, effective in 1978
Since 1980s	All states allow in-state branching New York, North Carolina, Maryland, and Rhode Island allow interstate branching	All states allow interstate bank holding Federal laws allow interstate acquisition of failed or failing banks and thrifts (the Depository Institution Reform Act and Monetary Control Act of 1980; the Gain-St. Germain Act of 1982; the Competitive Equality Banking Act of 1987)
1994	Nationwide interstate branching, effective in 1997, states can opt out (the Interstate Banking and Interstate Branching Efficiency Act of 1994)	Nationwide interstate bank holding effective in 1995 (the Interstate Banking and Interstate Branching Efficiency Act of 1994)

was an informal form of multi-office banking where several banks were owned or controlled by the same individual(s), while the latter was a more formal structure of multi-office banking where a controlling organization, usually a holding company, holds controlling stock in the affiliate banks. Both chain and group banking had intra- and inter-state multiple banking operations. Chain banking eventually evolved into group banking (Miller 1990a) due to the latter's ability to raise capital in the financial market, and thus its growth is less constrained. The late 1920s saw the rapid expansion of group banking. The Banking Act of 1933 officially defined group banking as bank holding affiliates (later as bank holding companies) and imposed weak regulation on them. The Bank Holding Company Act of 1956 was designed to regulate further expansion of banking holding companies and to require the divestment of their nonbanking activities. The Douglas Amendment of the Act prohibited further bank holding company interstate acquisition unless the state involved authorized it by law. Thus the Act essentially eliminated the possibility of further interstate activities through bank holding since by that time none of the states had legislation concerning interstate bank holding activities. Thus, after leaving branch banking legislation in the hands of states, Congress left intercounty and interstate banking by bank holding companies to state legislation.

It was not until 1978 that Maine became the first to adopt legislation allowing interstate banking on a national reciprocal basis. New York and Alaska followed Maine in 1982. From 1983 to 1985, interstate banking activity accelerated with the creation of regional interstate banking pacts (Saer and Gregorash 1986; Miller 1990a). Each pact was comprised of a number of states that were geographically adjacent and/or contiguous. Several regional pacts formed during this period, these were the New England pact which including six New England states,[6] the Southeastern pact which comprised of Alabama, Arkansas, Florida, Georgia, Kentucky, Louisiana, Maryland, Mississippi, North Carolina, South Carolina, Tennessee, Virginia, Washington D.C. and West Virginia,[7] the Mid-central states pact which encompassed Illinois, Indiana, Kentucky, Missouri, Ohio, Virginia, and West Virginia,[8] and the West pact which included Alaska, Arizona, California, Hawaii, Idaho, Nevada, Oregon, Utah, and Washington.[9] The Garn-St. Germain Depository Institutions Act of 1982 authorized interstate acquisition of failed or failing banks and thrifts.

Prior to the 1994 Interstate Banking and Branching Act, all states had allowed some form of interstate banking through bank holding companies (GOA 1994; Kamerschen 1992; Kohn 1991). Among them, 13 states as well as the District of Columbia allowed nationwide interstate banking without limitation (Alaska, Arizona, Colorado, Idaho, Maine, Nevada, New Hampshire, New Mexico, Oklahoma, Oregon, Texas, Utah, and Wyoming); 21 states allowed nationwide interstate banking on a reciprocal basis (California, Connecticut, Delaware, Illinois, Indiana, Kentucky, Louisiana, Massachusetts, Michigan, Nebraska, New Jersey, New York, North Dakota, Ohio, Pennsylvania, Rhode Island, South Dakota, Tennessee, Vermont, Washington, and West Virginia); 16 states required regional reciprocity (Arkansas, Alabama, Florida, Georgia, Hawaii,[10] Iowa, Kansas, Missouri, Mississippi, Montana, North Carolina, South Carolina, Maryland, Minnesota, Virginia, and Wisconsin). Therefore, on the eve of the federal nationwide interstate banking legislation, regional interstate banking pacts no longer existed in most areas except in the Southeast and among certain states in the Midwest. Even within the southeastern banking pact, a few states had legislation in place that would allow more liberal interstate banking at a future time. For example, Alabama law would allow nationwide interstate banking in September, 1995; Florida legislation would permit nationwide reciprocal interstate banking in May, 1995; In North Carolina, nationwide reciprocal interstate banking would be allowed in July 1996. This indicates that 37 states plus Washington DC had legislation permitting nationwide interstate banking. The time for strong federal action on interstate banking seems ripe.

The Riegle-Neal Interstate Banking and Branching Efficiency Act of 1994 is a landmark federal banking legislation. The Act essentially repeals the federal restrictions on interstate banking as embodied in the McFadden Act of 1927 and repeals the restrictions on interstate branching contained in the Douglas Amendment of the Bank Holding Company Act of 1956. According to the 1994 Act, nationwide interstate banking is allowed as of September, 1995, and nationwide interstate branching will be allowed, effective in July, 1997. A minor reservation to a full fledged free banking system is that this legislation allows states to opt out of interstate branching. Nonetheless, the 1994 Act has opened a new era of interstate banking operation in the United States. It is a major step by which the federal government takes back from the states the power to define the geographic extent for banking expansion. It is the first time in U.S. federal banking legislation history that a strong federal banking law emerges systematically addressing the geographic issues that had been over looked for too long. Its impacts on the U. S. banking industry and banking geography will be seen for years to come.

NOTES

1. National banks receive their charters from the Comptroller of the Currency of the U.S. Treasury Department while state banks receive charters from state banking authorities.

2. There are two grandfathered exceptions: The San Francisco based Bank of California, N.A. has branches in Oregon and Washington; and the New Jersey based Heritage Bank has branches in Pennsylvania.

3. Statewide branching is allowed as of January, 1997.

4. Statewide *de novo* branching is allowed as of January, 1999.

5. Specific types of limitations include: (a). Locations of branches are required to be confined within the city or county where the head office is located, within the counties contiguous to the head office county, or within a certain distance from the head office; (b). The numbers of branches are set for the head office county, contiguous counties, or cities of various sizes; (c). Capital requirements for branch banks.

6. Not all states within a regional pact have similar legislation. For example, by April 1985, of the six New England states, Maine allowed nationwide non-reciprocal banking, New Hampshire and Vermont had not yet passed interstate banking legislation, and Rhode Island, Massachusetts, and Connecticut had regional reciprocal legislation. Therefore, the extent of the New England pact was defined by inclusion of all states that were permitted banking entry by the last three states.

7. In 1985, not all Southeastern states had the same definition concerning the extent of the Southeastern banking pact. This list reflects the states that were within the Southeastern pact well established during the early 1990s.

8. Note that Kentucky, Virginia, and West Virginia were part of both the Southeastern and Mid-central pacts. By the early 1990s, the Mid-central pact was replaced by the Midwest pact. The extent of the Midwest pact varied among states. According to the frequency of occurrence in states' definitions, the following states were mentioned

by at least three states as included in this pact: Iowa, Illinois, Indiana, Kansas, Kentucky, Minnesota, Missouri, Nebraska, and Wisconsin.

9. This list only reflects Oregon's definition of the West pact. Other states normally have a much narrower definition. By the early 1990s, the West pact disappeared since most western states adopted nationwide interstate banking law.

10. Regional reciprocity with Guam, American Samoa, the Northern Mariarans, the Marshall Islands, Micronesia and Palau.

III

Literature Review

This chapter provides a review of existing studies concerning firm location theory, banking production functions, multi-location production functions, the theoretical foundation of the spatial interaction model, geographic distribution of banking place networks, and banking performance analysis. The purpose is not to provide an exhaustive review of the literature but to disentangle the theoretical issues involved in banking geographical operations and to point out problems in existing studies.

PRODUCTION FUNCTION AND FIRM LOCATION THEORY

In the theory of production, the concept of a firm is succinctly expressed as a production function where certain inputs are organized to produce a certain output. A textbook firm faces the problem of deciding the optimal level of output and combination of inputs. The issue of location has been ignored for a long time (Isard 1956). Early efforts to address the issue of firm location were conducted independent of the theory of the firm. Most important were von Thünen's agricultural location theory and Weber's industrial location theory (Weber 1957; Thünen 1826).

The von Thünen theory addresses the issue of the spatial pattern of crop raising surrounding a city. Farming firms are assumed to use the Leontief technology. That is, the proportion of inputs is fixed and independent of location. Under such assumptions, the differential bid-rent is equal to the differential transport cost between any two locations. For a given output level, land use intensity is identical at various locations. The same technology is assumed in Weber's theory, which addresses the issue of the optimal location for an industrial firm. For a given output level, the optimal location is determined by the least cost location within a location triangle or a location polygon.

These classical firm location issues have been generalized within neoclassical microeconomics by contemporary location theorists. Moses (1958) initiated the application of the theory of production in the classical Weber problem, and was followed by Emerson (1973), Mai (1981), and Part and Mathur (1988), among others. The result is a generalized Weber problem where the optimal level of output, optimal input combination, and optimal firm location are determined simultaneously. For a given output, the optimal location is described by an arc within the location triangle. Each point on the arc represents a different input combination. Different output results in a different arc. In land use study, Alonso (1964) and Muth (1961) were among the first to apply microeconomic consumer theory in a residential land use study. In the Alonso-Muth framework, land is treated as one of the goods consumed by the consumer. The optimal level of utility is reached where the amount of land consumed and associated land use location, and the amount of other goods are in equilibrium. Due to many parallel aspects of consumer and production theories, conclusions from the Alonso-Muth framework can be easily extended into agricultural land use (Fujita 1984). Thus the classical von Thünen problem is extended into the generalized von Thünen problem, where the bid-rent curve is a curve and bid-rent differential is not necessarily the same as the differential transport cost between any two locations. In addition, land use intensity varies spatially according to changing land price and input substitution. Thus, economic activities with different resource use intensities are carried out at different distances away from a central city. The central market serves as a trading spot between firms in different rings. This latter result contains the essential concept of neoclassical comparative advantage (Samuelson 1978) that was found in Heckscher-Ohlin factor proportion theory (Ohlin 1933). Therefore, the study of firm location adds to the understanding of division of labor in a spatial context.

While agricultural and industrial firm location problems are dealt with under the classical/generalized von Thünen/Weber problems, the service firm location issue is generally considered to be dealt with within central place theory (Wheeler and Mitchelson 1989). Christaller's classical central place theory was developed independently of neoclassical microeconomics (Christaller 1966). Lösch (1954) was the first to apply neoclassical market theory in the study of central place issues and proved that a central place/market area system was a special case of the monopolistic competition model, a landmark market model in economics, developed by Chamberlin (1932) and Robinson (1933). Lösch's study established a close connection between central place study and neoclassical economics, and nurtured later spatial monopolistic study by Greenhut (Greenhut *et al.* 1975; 1987), among others. The study of central place in general has also nurtured service location research such as urban retail networks (Berry and Pred 1961).

Central place theory addresses certain service firm location issues, such as market area determination. Thus it provides a conceptual framework for certain retail activities including retail banking (Bennett 1975; Lundsten 1978). However, central place theory does not explicitly address the issue of the resource allocation process within a service firm. Input substitution is generally missing in most central place and related retail activity studies. Therefore, service firms in the central place system can only be seen as using the Leontief technology. In light of generalized von Thünen/Weber problems, a Leontief production function for a service firm is too restrictive.

PRODUCTION FUNCTION FOR BANKING FIRMS

Much confusion exists in constructing production functions for banking firms. A major problem seems to originate in disagreement among researchers concerning what constitutes a banking firm's output and input (Sealey and Lindley 1977). Five categories of banking output have been used. The first is value added, which is similar to the widely used measure of aggregate manufacturing output. For example, the Office of Business Economics, U.S. Commerce Department, defines the output from the banking sector as total property income, the net of interest paid, plus service charges (Marimont 1969). The second category of banking output is defined as the number of accounts served by a bank, an analog to the physical amount of output. Such a definition is considered to be a counterpart of the textbook production function in which output is usually a physical amount (Benston 1965; Benston *et al.* 1982). The third category involves the dollar volume of deposit accounts (Longbrake and Haslem 1975). The fourth output category is the dollar volume of total assets or earning assets. For example, Clark (1984) treated total loanable funds as output. Gropper

(1991) used the total dollar volume in investment, total loans, and trust accounts as a measure of output. Finally, the dollar volume of earning assets and deposits are together used as a measure of output. Examples of its use include Gilligan and Smirlock (1984), Hunter and Timme (1986), Buono and Eakin (1990), and Berger and Humphrey (1991). As for inputs, most researchers adopt conventional input categories such as labor and capital. However, the status of deposits is less clear. On the one hand, deposits and earning assets are entries on the opposite side in a banking firm's balance sheet, i.e., liabilities and assets. This results in the impression of deposits as an input in producing earning assets (Sealey and Lindley 1977). On the other hand, banking firms incur costs such as wages and interest to attract deposits from customers. This process differs little from producing a normal output. Sealey and Lindley (1977) conceptually solved the dilemma concerning what constitutes banking output and input. They proposed a multiple stage production process for banking firms. A banking firm is perceived to use labor and capital to take deposits and deposits, labor, and capital are then used to produce earning assets. This proposal does not only clarify the confusion pertaining to banking outputs and inputs, but also provides new insight concerning the operational mechanism of a banking firm. What is missing in their proposal is a concrete functional form that contains this multiple stage banking process.

PRODUCTION FUNCTION AND MULTI-LOCATION OPERATION

Compared with the volume of literature that addresses classical/neoclassical firm location issues where the firm concerned has only a unitary operating location, the production function with multiple locations has received much less treatment. Although the general notion of achieving the identical marginal productivity among all branches is well established (Li 1987), the locational/network pattern of the firm's operating units are often not the focus in most textbook production functions.

Fujita (1981) is one of the very few locational theorists who explicitly addresses the multi-location issue under the classical/neoclassical location theory framework. He adopts the conventional location triangle and discusses the process where two firms (firms 3 and 4 in Fujita's notation) within the location triangle with input transactions achieve optimal location. He first looks at the problem of obtaining equilibrium locations for the two firms under the assumption that the two firms are independently managed. For any location of firm 3, the first-order condition of a production function gives an equilibrium location for firm 4 as in the classical Weber problem; for any location of firm 4, the first-order condition gives an equilibrium location for firm 3, such that there are an unlimited number of equilibrium location pairs for the two firms. Which is the actual equilibrium pair depends on the historical and dynamic background. He then assumes common ownership of the two firms and solves for the classical Weber problem where the total transport cost for the pair is a minimum. The optimal locational pair from such a solution does not coincide with the equilibrium pair. Although Fujita's conceptual framework can theoretically be extended to situations where more than two locations are involved, the unlimited possible set of locations of all firms involved generates great difficulty in obtaining meaningful solutions. Two additional problems with this approach are that the firms are assumed to use Leontief technology; and the two firms are of separate production functions. In this regard, this is not a truly generalized model for firms with multi-location operations.

With the neoclassical production framework, multi-unit firm issues are widely discussed within the framework of industrial organization economics. The main emphasis is how different types of markets (e.g., perfectly competitive, or competitively monopolistic) in up-stream or down-stream stages of production cause integration or disintegration of firms (Schmalensee *et al.* 1989). The location is not necessarily a main focus though it may become an issue where a certain type of market exists due to locational conditions. For example, a firm occupying a location alone forms a local monopoly and thus becomes a target of integration in competition for local monopolistic profits (Blair and Kaserman 1985). Thus, market type, instead of production function, is the major focus in this line of research.

Recent years have seen important developments in the field of industrial organization economics concerning the multi-location issue. Panzar and Willig (1977), and Baumol, Panzar, and Willig (1982) theoretically established the notion of economies of scope, where the total cost of producing multiple outputs within one single firm is lower than the sum of the costs when these outputs are produced by separate firms. This notion has been generalized to include all multiple operations, either in terms of products or locations (Bailey and Fiedlaender 1982; Brander and Eaton 1984; Anderson 1985 1987; Archibald *et al*. 1986; Anderson *et al*. 1989; Thill 1992). In a spatial context, the analogy of economies of scope is the advantage associated with multi-location operation. Although a neoclassical type of production function is not explicitly contained in models, this generalization provides an important, uniform conceptual foundation to treat the issue of industrial and spatial structures. In addition, the equilibrium industrial/locational structure achieved through interaction between cost functions and demand functions provides a novel angle from which to view the multi-location issue.

An important field of study that has experienced rapid development in recent decades and has shed light on spatial analysis is transaction economics. Transaction economics provides a supplemental, instead of competing, theoretical tool in analyzing firm organization (Arrow *et al*. 1982). Transaction economics sees transaction cost as a key factor in determining the forms of division of labor: market verses firms (Coase 1939; Williamson 1975; 1986). An extension of this conceptual framework in a spatial context is to see a certain type of firm headquarters-subsidiary-branch network as a result of transaction cost that exists among various locations. Scott (1988) has used such a framework when investigating firm integration/disintegration in a spatial context. In his study, the cost resulting from a production function and transaction cost coexist to determine the form of firms.

The multi-location issue is also dealt with by the neoclassical location theorists in a more sophisticated field: the general equilibrium location study. The division of partial and general equilibrium location theories is based on the theoretical differences between partial and general equilibrium studies in neoclassical economics, which are based on the Marshall (1920) partial equilibrium, and the Walras (1954) and Debreu (1959) general equilibrium theories respectively. Thus, partial equilibrium location theory seeks optimal location for a particular industry or firm, given locations of all other industries and firms. The conventional von Thünen and Weber problems all belong to this field. The general equilibrium location theory seeks locational pattern where locations for all industries and firms, and for all factors of production, are allowed to change (Fujita 1990). An early attempt to address the general location-equilibrium problem was made by Schweizer *et al*. (1976) using a spatial Walrasian model. Fujita (1990) summarized four possible types of general location-equilibrium model: Type A, a neoclassical version of comparative advantage models (Ohlin 1933), as a revision to the classical Ricardian trade theory (1911), where factors are assumed to be immobile between locations while products are spatially mobile; Type B, nonprice interaction models where the focus is how contact among economic agents (firms and households) and agglomeration affect equilibrium locations of economic agents (Beckmann 1976); Type C, monopolistic competition models which are a generalized spatial version of the Chamberlinian monopolistic competition model (Fujita 1988); and Type D, oligopolistic interaction models, which are a spatial version of different oligopolistic competition models (Sakashita 1987; Fujita and Thisse 1987). In all these models, firm headquarters and branches are assumed to have separate production functions. This provides convenience in deriving equilibrium solutions. However, the possibility of a multi-stage production process within a banking firm suggested by Sealey and Lindley (1971) is ruled out. In addition, these models implicitly suggest that each (or each group of) product is represented by one production function. As a result, the explicit expression of multi-output nature of a firm is missing (Fujita 1990).

PRODUCTION FUNCTION AND BANKING PERFORMANCE ASSESSMENT

Industrial performance study is theoretically consistent with production function theory and related cost theory. From the production theory point of view, firm operational efficiency can be described by technical efficiency and allocative efficiency (Lovell and Sickles 1983; Morrison 1993). Technical efficiency refers to the ability to achieve the maximum level of output with available inputs. Allocative efficiency means producing a given level of output at the minimum cost. The measurement of allocative efficiency is conducted under a general area of study: the measurement of total factor productivity. The measurement of technical efficiency is captured by the measurement of capacity utilization. For a long time, economists have been interested in measuring variations in total output that cannot be explained by variations in the factors of production. Early measurement was conducted by using various index numbers such as the Divisia index, or the Törnqvist index for discrete data (Törnqvist 1936). Since

Solow's groundbreaking work (1957), researchers have found a close relationship between index numbers and the theory of production. Solow decomposed a change in total output into changes associated with the amount of various factors of production used and changes associated with time. Since between two points in time, even the same amount of various inputs can produce different levels of output, the output differential can only be attributed to the technical changes that occur during the interval. The output increase associated with technical change is defined as total factor productivity. Solow showed that within the neoclassical production function framework, this approach is equivalent to the index number approach (Jorgensen *et al.* 1978; Caves *et al.* 1982). Denny and Fuss (1983) generalized Solow's theory so that both variations associated with time and variations associated with distance can be measured. The former is termed the Intertemporal index number and the latter the Interspatial index number.

The Solow/index number framework essentially uses an accounting procedure. That is, a change in total output is seen as a sum of changes associated with different factors of production plus changes associated with technical changes. The effect of variations in labor productivity on production is therefore a special case when capital is assumed to be a constant (Morrison 1993). This notion can be extended into situations where more than one input are variable. When all inputs and their substitution are considered, the total factor productivity notion results. Similar notions can be expressed with a cost function. Duality theory states that for any production function, a minimum cost function exists as long as certain regularity conditions are met (Shephard 1953; Diewert 1971). A cost function is generally expressed as a function of total output and input prices (Watt 1980; Silberberg 1990). Therefore, the cost differential that cannot be explained by output differential, and input price differentials, is attributed to variations in productivity (Morrison 1993). Under conventional neoclassical production theory, the separability and linear output or cost elasticities (homogeneity) are always assumed. Under these assumptions, parameters in the these accounting procedures are factor shares in total output. Information concerning these categories is readily available. Thus no statistical estimation is necessary (Jorgensen *et al.* 1978; Denny and Fuss 1983).

Recent decades have seen a generalization of this approach into the generalized flexible production function. A flexible production function can be defined as a second order Taylor expansion for any input/output relationship (Berndt and Christensen 1973; Christensen *et al.* 1973). The advantage of flexible function forms is that no assumptions are made on the functional behavior and that various neoclassical assumptions can be treated as constraints on the functional parameters (Christensen *et al.* 1973; Murphy and White 1983). Diewert (1976) and Denny and Fuss (1983) have shown that when constraints on these parameters take different values, the flexible function can be reduced to a neoclassical production function. The widely used Cobb-Douglas and Constant Elasticity of Substitution production functions are special cases of the flexible form (Christensen *et al.* 1973; Kolari *et al.* 1987). With generalized flexible production functions, the parameters, which are the first- and second-order derivatives of a Taylor expansion, must be statistically estimated in order to obtain the measurement of productivity (Jorgensen *et al.* 1978; Denny and Fuss 1983). The same principles apply to flexible cost functions (Morrison 1993).

Total factor productivity is a residual term in the total variations in total output, which may contain a variety of elements such as technical change, economies of scale and structure elements that are not explicitly contained in the functions (Solow 1957). The estimation of economies of scale in banking firms has generated an enormous amount of literature which use both neoclassical functional forms (Benston 1972; Longbrake and Haslem 1975) and, more recently, flexible forms (Benston *et al.* 1982). More frequently cost functions were estimated since it is possible to incorporate multi-output in estimation (Murphy and White 1983; Gilligan *et al.* 1984; Hunter and Timme 1985). The general motivation is to investigate how output changes with inputs (production functions) or how cost changes with input prices and output cost functions. A less than proportional increase in output to an increase in inputs, or a more than proportional increase in cost to an increase in outputs are said to indicate the existence of diseconomies of scale. Otherwise, economies of scale are said to exist.

Following Panzar and Willig's work (1977), some researchers began to incorporate economies of scope in the measurement of economies of scale in banking performance. The results are mixed. Some find evidence of economies of scale (Benston 1982; Gilligan *et al.* 1984); others disputed the concept of economies of scale in banking operations (Boyd and Graham 1991). From a geographical point of view, many results are questionable in that most of these studies have been conducted without controlling for spatial and hierarchical variations. The fact that the most work in this area has been done by economists may explain this lack of emphasis on geographic elements. However, there is indeed an issue of how to incorporate spatial and hierarchical structures into estimation. Spatial and hierarchical structures are usually not readily observable and quantifiable variables. Estimation of their effects on banking performance may not easily be made directly.

Morrison (1993) has shown that the measurement of technical efficiency can be conducted with measurement of capacity utilization. That is, to calculate the ratio between actual output to the optimal output with available inputs. Conceptually, this approach consists of the estimation of the tangent point between long-run and short-run cost curves. The difference between the two cost curves is that the former contains certain fixed inputs as arguments. Such a tangent point gives the optimal output where the short-run shadow-value of any fixed input equals the market price of the input. With estimated optimal output and observed output, the ratio can be constructed. A ratio greater than one indicates that the fixed input involved is overutilized; otherwise it is underutilized. A dual approach in estimating capacity utilization is to estimate the ratio between the shadow value of the fixed input and its market price.

The above development in the analytical study of banking performance has occurred amid changes in banking legislation pertaining to banking geographic expansion, and resultant changes in banking structure. These new methods are designed to provide rigorous empirical tests on issues concerning banking structure and performance, including the impact of interstate banking on banking concentration and competition (Holly 1987), the viability of small banks (Frieder *et al*. 1985), banking profitability, safety and stability (Eisenbeis 1985), and banking efficiency (Benston 1985). A common flaw in these studies is a lack of geographical elements while discussing geographically related issues. Geographic expansion through branching and bank holding companies have various patterns. Some bank holding companies expand to neighboring states while others leap-frog to nonadjacent states. Some spread their bank affiliation networks all over the country while others expand only within regional or even state boundaries. Some conduct their business in major metropolitan areas while others operate in smaller metropolitan areas. Existing banking performance study has mostly ignored these specific patterns of spatial operation and brought them under a uniform form: size expansion. Therefore interstate banking, or multi-locational banking operation has been practically simplified as a study between bank size and banking performance. The possible impact on bank operation of various firm networks or various external environments has been ignored, or at least, simplified without empirical testing.

Furthermore, much of current research has treated intercounty and interstate banking expansion by bank holding companies as *de facto* intercounty and interstate branch banking (Compton 1987). Researchers have frequently brought up banking structure in other countries, such as Canada and Japan, as a comparable reference in discussing changes in the U.S. banking system. A study of this nature has ignored a basic fact: a bank holding company is legally not a bank. It is a network of affiliated banks that are connected through property ownership. A bank holding company may influence affiliated banks in many ways, such as through the election of the board of directors of affiliated banks via its voting stock, or through issuance of better reputed stock or securities to acquire funds and subsequent lending to affiliated banks. Nonetheless, banks under a bank holding company are still independently incorporated entities. For state charted banks that are under the same bank holding company, various banks are even under different state regulatory authorities. More importantly, various federal or state banking regulations are bank specific or bank holding company specific. These regulations may cause very different responses from different forms of banking organization and, therefore, may generate different levels of efficiency.

In addition, although the level of control of a bank holding company over its affiliated banks varies, generally speaking, affiliated banks under a bank holding company enjoy much more autonomy than branches under a bank (Bonbright and Means 1969; Rose 1989). Various studies have shown that the development of bank holding companies is partly a response to the various regulations on banks in attempt to get around regulatory restraints ranging from product supply to branch banking (Bonbright and Means 1969; Haywood 1973; Cartinhour and Westerfield 1981). Such a substitution of a spatial network of affiliated banks for a branch network may not necessarily be perfect. In fact, evidence has shown that bank holding companies are usually the first stage of amalgamation in which separate banks fuse into a single entity (Fischer 1961; Bonbright and Means 1969). Some researchers anticipate full interstate banking by allowing branch banking across state lines (Mengle 1989; 1990) as a continuation of changes accommodating banking spatial requirements. The dichotomous attitudes long held by state legislatures toward branch banking and interstate bank holding is clear evidence that these are two distinctly different organizational configurations. Such differences have largely been ignored in most recent empirical studies on multi-location banking.

PRODUCTION FUNCTIONS AND THEORETICAL FOUNDATION OF THE SPATIAL INTERACTION MODEL

Although conventional partial equilibrium firm location theory is important in understanding the geographic distribution of economic activities, it is less than satisfactory in describing the aggregate spatial configuration of economic landscapes. This is because of its emphasis on certain segments of economic activities, either certain firms in an industry, or certain industries in the overall economy. Thus, in describing the aggregate spatial configuration of the economic landscape, economic geographers have chosen the spatial interaction model.

The spatial interaction model in social sciences is analogous to, and originally derived from, the Newtonian laws of force and energy. It recognizes the association between the degree of spatial interaction on the one hand, and the magnitude of economic activities found at places and distance between places, one the other. Early social physicists adopted the gravity model, similar to its original form in physics, in studies ranging from migration to retail market, trade, population distribution and settlement patterns (Carey 1858; Reilly 1929; Anderson 1955; Carrothers 1956). The early models generally used place population as estimates of propulsive and attractive power and physical distance as the magnitude of separation. From early gravity models have developed important variations (Haynes and Fotheringham 1984). For example, the potential model generalizes the model that describes flows between a pair of places into the one that describes flows among all places in a system. Place propulsive and attractive power have been explicitly linked to specific place attributes that are conceived to directly affect the trip-making decision in particular journeys such a retail shopping (Huff 1960; Young 1975; Nourse 1990). In addition to distance, intervening opportunities and their possible competitive or agglomerative effects on interaction have also been incorporated into the model (Fotheringham 1983). Furthermore, Huff (1963) initiated the conceptual breakthrough of recasting the gravity model from a deterministic to a probabilistic perspective. Distance is considered to have diminishing effect on trip probability, and trip patterns are regarded as independent probabilistic realizations of distance-aversion behavior (Smith 1978). Based on information on types of flows, the gravity model expands to a family of models such as the total flow constrained model, the production constrained model, the attraction constrained model, and the doubly constrained model (Lowry 1964; Wilson 1971; Haynes and Fotheringham 1984). Finally, according to the nature of flow origin or destination, there are divisions of traditional models where multiple origins and destinations exist, origin-specific models where one origin and multiple destinations exist, and destination specific models where multiple origins and one destination exist. The combination of such systems with gravity family models generate a wider range and variety of spatial interaction models (Haynes and Fotheringham 1984).

In spite of its wide use and powerful influence in many geographical studies, the spatial interaction model in economic geography literature generally suffers from a lack of rigorous analytical foundation, as pointed out by Niedercorn and Bechdolt (1969), and thus has unidentified properties (Anderson 1979). Although Ullman's triad (1945) is considered to provide a theoretical basis for spatial interaction (Krmenec 1993), such interpretation is far from rigorous. Some important elements in the triad are directly borrowed from economic theory. For example, the concept of complementarity is borrowed from neoclassical trade theory, and transferability is borrowed from the analysis of tariff/distance effects on trade. However, the rigor of the neoclassical trade theory disappears in the gravity model. The behavioral functions that describe supply and demand are submerged under aggregate flow functions. The process of transition from a micro-level mechanism to macro-level flows is more intuitively rather than analytically clear.

While geographers emphasize the operational rigor of the gravity model, some economists attempt to provide a microeconomic foundation for the model. That is, they see the gravity model as an aggregate result of individual or community decision-making. Thus, such an aggregate model should be derived from micro-level behavioral functions.

One early attempt in this direction was made by Niedercorn and Bechdolt (1969). They derived the gravity model in a household trip-making decision making setting. A separable utility function is assumed which contains utility obtainable from different destinations. The first-order condition generates the optimal allocation among alternative destinations. The summation of such trip allocations of all individuals produces a gravity model. Anderson (1979) derived the gravity model from expenditures on trade goods. Given a country's or region's shares of total expenditures on imports from each other, equality is established between a country or region's imports and exports. The expenditure is partially affected by the landed value of import products, which is a function of tariff rates and transport rates. A certain derivation generates a trade flow equation where trading amounts between countries or regions are positively correlated with the size of total expenditure and negatively correlated with tariff/transport rates. Such a notion is quite familiar in regional macroeconomic trade analysis (Richardson 1979).

One important microeconomic conceptual foundation for the gravity model is found in general equilibrium settings. Linnemann (1966) used a Walras general equilibrium model to express the determination of the gravity model. A set of demand functions contains total income, prices, and import transport costs as exogenous. A set of supply functions contains prices and total production capacity as exogenous. The interaction between demand and supply generates a turnover function (Tinbergen 1962) which expresses the equilibrium supply/demand. This is actually the trade flow equation expressed as a function of transport costs and total income level. Such a gravity model based on general equilibrium theory is further developed by Bergstrand (1985). He used a neoclassical Constant Elasticity of Substitution (CES) production function and a Constant Elasticity Transformation (CET) utility function in a general equilibrium setting. The adoption of specific functional forms allowed him to obtain a solution to the trade flow argument. The result is a generalized gravity model where functional parameters vary across countries depending on parameters of a countries' utility and production functions. Compared with the original notion behind the gravity model, the general equilibrium framework deals with supply and demand simultaneously and thus provides a much more promising possibility to provide a rigorous theoretical foundation for the gravity model to describe the aggregate spatial configuration of economic flows.

STUDY OF THE ECONOMIC LANDSCAPE OF BANKING CORPORATE NETWORK

In the past two decades, corporate geography has become an important branch of contemporary economic geography. Generally, corporate geography is concerned with locations of decision-making units and related producer services (Semple and Phipps 1982). Banking corporations, with their geographically bounded network and active role in corporate financing, constitute an important area in the study of corporate geography.

One important research area in current banking corporate geography is the examination of the metropolitan concentration of the banking industry. Various studies have examined the close relationship between banking and other economic sectors (Updike 1988; Gourgues and Lauterbach 1987; Kinderberger 1983; South and Poston 1982). This relationship materializes as industrial and commercial loans offered by banks to firms in other sectors. The potential default by borrowing institutions brings credit risk to banks. This requires banks to locate their loan facilities close by the headquarters of their institutional customers so that banks can monitor and evaluate customers' performance. The ultimate goal is to reduce default risk. Such geographic proximity is important in that since most industrial and commercial loans are short-term in nature, and rollover is almost routine (Sinkey 1983; Graddy and Spencer 1990). Constant monitoring of the customers' performance becomes basic strategy in reducing default risk. Since major corporations tend to headquarter in large metropolitan areas (Semple and Phipps 1982; Wheeler 1986; Ross 1992), the tendency for banking activity to concentrate in metropolitan areas is a natural result of the effort to reduce transaction costs. Such geographic proximity between banks and corporate headquarters are captured in the Stanback and Noyelle (1982) hypothesis on locational behavior of producer services (including banks). Laderman *et al.* (1991) provide evidence showing that the bank monitoring cost increases with distance. In addition, the monetary function requires close proximity between banks and customers including both institutions and individuals. Wheeler and Dillon (1985) have proved the significant spatial relationship between corporate prominence and population, on the one hand, and banking activity on the other.

The study of the metropolitan concentration of the banking industry often constitutes the foundation for another important area in banking geography study: the study of banking command/control fields. Command/control functions between places are exerted by corporate organizations that operate in multiple locations (Clarke 1985). Borchert (1972; 1978) was among the earliest to examine the spatial banking linkages that form in corporate business relationships such as correspondent banking. Wheeler (1988) pioneered the use of command/control indices (such as C-value and D-value) to depict a place's position in the corporate command/control network. Generally speaking, the place that generates more out-reaching than in-coming ownerships in the corporate network is considered to be in a command and control position (Wheeler 1988; Wheeler and Mitchelson 1989). Such indices conceptually establish the notion of command and control. Ross (1992) also contributed to the notion of corporate command/control by emphasizing that since command and control are exerted by corporations, the study of spatial networks must give more attention to corporations themselves. This constitutes a micro-level examination of the spatial behavior of banking activity and financial resources. Later research adopts corporate ownership as an indication of the magnitude of corporate command/control. For example, Lord (1992) examined the changes of corporate ownership in total banking assets since banking deregulation, and found rapid concentration of such ownership in several major metropolitan areas and states.

One problem in studies of banking command/control is the lack of a concrete place network formed on a banking firm ownership network basis. According to Rose, the hierarchical command/control relationship between places is mainly formed on the basis of corporate ownership. Wheeler's command/control indices also clearly contain such a notion. In most current banking geography studies, however, the total banking financial assets (either banking assets or deposits) that are held by banking institutions (both head and branch offices) are often used as a surrogate for magnitude of influence (Wheeler and Dillon 1986; Wheeler and Zhou 1994). This measure may be misleading because some offices and their financial holdings in a particular place are owned by banks or bank holding companies outside that place. Therefore, the magnitude of this portion of financial holding is not a measure of command/control of a place but, on the contrary, is a measure of being commanded/controlled. Similarly, Lord (1992) used ownership of banking assets by banks and bank holding companies in a particular place as a measure of the magnitude of dominance of that place but failed to identify the location of assets owned. In short, in the current banking corporate landscape study, the geographical extent of a place in the banking command/control field based on spatial banking linkages has not been identified. The hierarchical structure of the banking command/control field can only be approximated by using the total financial holdings of various places. The specific hierarchical dominance/subordination relationship based on banking ownership between places has never been systematically revealed.

Another problem within current banking corporate geography is the lack of distinction between branching networks and bank holding networks. That is, different types of spatial ownership and command/control networks have never been separately identified. Geographical banking linkages based on branch ownership concern a lower level of ownership compared with that under banking holding company ownership. A command/control center in the branch banking field may have a substantial portion of its banking assets commanded and controlled by bank holding companies located in other places. As a result, this center is more likely to be subordinate in the bank holding field. In general, a dominant center in the branch ownership field may not necessarily be dominant in the bank holding ownership field. Only at those centers that are dominant in bank holding ownership is the highest level of decision-making conducted. Such centers thus possess the greatest dominance. In other words, there are different layers of dominance and command/control functions related to different levels of decision-making functions in banking organizations. The most dominant centers are likely to be those that are dominant centers in the highest banking decision-making functions. Without disentangling branch dominance from bank holding dominance and basing banking dominance only on the aggregate banking assets, the nature of the place in actual banking command and control networks may not be clearly seen.

CONCLUDING REMARKS

The above review of the banking study literature has indicated several important voids in current banking geography study. The first is a lack of an analytical framework for banking firm operations that are essentially multi-input, multi-output, multi-stage, and multi-location. Secondly, the there is also a lack of analytical foundation in conceptualizing spatial configurations of banking networks based on the spatial interaction of banking activities. In addition, the empirical study of banking geography is also handicapped due to meager past attention to the banking corporate landscape based on corporate ownership. Finally, banking performance study is generally conducted in an aspatial context. These unaddressed issues point to new areas for banking geography study and it is to these that the next three chapters will turn.

IV

Mechanisms Of Banking Operation
In a Spatial Context

This chapter gives a theoretical account of micro-level and macro-level mechanisms concerning the spatial behavior of banking firms and the banking industry. Specifically, for the firm-level, a production function of multi-output, multi-input, multi-stage and multi-location is derived. The purpose is to establish an equilibrium solution for a banking firm in a spatial context. The emphasis is on the resource allocation mechanism for a banking firm that possesses a spatial network. Such a network contains both internal and external spatial elements as discussed in Chapter I. The internal elements refer to the multi-location characteristics for a generalized banking firm. The external elements indicate the economic environment, especially urban economies. The process of resource allocation is seen as an equilibrium among decisions concerning input level, output level, and the locational network.

The macro-level mechanism here refers to the process in which communities interact to form banking ties and banking place networks across communities. A simple general equilibrium system is applied to derive banking owning networks across communities. In addition, a system of community utility functions is used to derive bank owning networks among communities. Both models can be transformed to a generalized gravity model. Thus, the macro-level mechanism to be derived can be seen to provide a microeconomic foundation for the gravity model.

The first section derives a multi-stage and multi-location production function for banking firms. The second section, based on the function derived, analyzes banking firms' behavior in a spatial context, i.e., the optimal resource allocation in a multi-locational setting. The third section is devoted to a derivation of the macro-mechanism of spatial bank asset holding. The last section draws conclusions from the models derived.

A BANKING FIRM PRODUCTION FUNCTION

This section derives a multi-input, multi-output, multi-stage, and multi-location production function for banking firms. The organization of the section is as follows. The aggregation mechanism of production functions is first briefly discussed. A presentation of multi-stage banking production function and its behavioral properties is then made. This function is then extended into a multi-locational form. The discussion within this section establishes the foundation for the banking conduct analysis contained in the next section.

Separability and Aggregation of Production Functions

A production function expresses the quantitative relationship between inputs and outputs, i.e., the maximum amount of various physical outputs that can be produced by a certain amount of various physical inputs. A typical textbook production function usually includes one output Y, and two inputs, labor N, and capital K, i.e., $Y=f(N, K)$. This is an overly simplified function, since various types of labor and capital used in the production process are represented by only two inputs in the function. In the context of banking firms, this means that tellers, accountants, managers at various levels, and executives are lumped together under "labor," while furniture, computer and electronic facilities, and office space are lumped together under "capital." In principle, each of these items, or even each individual worker or each individual facility plays a more or less differentiated role in a banking firm. Therefore, each can be listed as one input in the production function. As Wallis (1980) pointed out, it is only at a level of an individual or piece of machinery that factors can be viewed as nonseparable. However, to use available aggregated data and make a production function mathematically manageable, a certain aggregation is necessary. That is, certain indexes must be introduced that express the roles played by a diversified pool of inputs. This transformation is made possible by introducing the concept of separability with respect to the behavior of variables, a strong assumption put forth initially by

Leontief (1947), and subsequently developed by researchers such as Goldman and Uzawa (1964) and Solow (1965).

Separability means that the marginal rate of substitution between two variables is independent of other variables, a necessary condition for aggregation (Goldman and Uzawa 1964). With the separability assumption, bottom-up aggregation is possible. Through indexing the effect of a certain number of inputs using a transformation, the number of inputs in the function is reduced. The resultant indices can also be indexed through further transformation, reducing the number of inputs even further. This process can continue until the degree of aggregation reaches a point where relevant aggregated data are available, and the number of input indexes in the function become manageable. The same principle applies in the treatment of outputs, indexing multiple outputs with a single aggregated output index. The significance of separability is that the aggregator functions retain the major characteristics of the well-behaved micro-function, such as monotone, convexity, and diminishing marginal productivity.

Multi-Stage Banking Firm Production Function

Suppose that a general aggregated production function for a banking firm is expressed as follows:

$$F(y_1, y_2, y_3, \ldots, y_n, x_1, x_2, x_3, \ldots, x_m) = 0 \qquad (4.1)$$

where y_i's $(i = 1, 2, \ldots, n)$ include all kinds of outputs produced and x_j's $(j = 1, 2, \ldots, m)$ include all inputs used. These outputs and inputs should reflect the level of aggregation so that values in the function are observable aggregates in the income statement and balance sheet of a banking firm. Specifically, the major aggregates frequently mentioned in the literature include labor, capital, loans (commercial and industrial, personal, and real estate), securities investments, deposits (transaction and nontransaction accounts), and total income. Chapter III has discussed a variety of functional forms used in describing the banking production process. The above variables occur in some functional forms but are missing in others. These different forms essentially describe different aspects of banking operations. There is a need to systematically organize these different forms so that the relationship between them can be seen.

Sealey and Lindley (1977) proposed a multistage concept for banking firms. They contended that deposits are intermediate outputs of a banking firm. The deposits will, along with real resources such as labor and capital, be used to produce earning assets. Following this logic, this research proposes a production function with three layers of aggregation. Figure 4.1 shows a flow chart that depicts the conceptual logic behind these layers of aggregation. At the bottom are the *primary resources* of a banking firm, labor N and capital K. The primary resources are used to take deposits or other liability items. These items are uniformly expressed here with D, a financial resource for a banking firm. This constitutes a first-order transformation $D=d(N,K)$. After deposits are taken, they are used, along with the real resources of labor and capital, to produce loans L and other investment I. Sealey and Lindley argued convincingly for treating deposits as an input. Their major argument is that deposits act as a rented resource, with interest as an explicit cost, and safekeeping, check clearing, and bookkeeping as implicit costs. Therefore, there is a second-order transformation $X=x(D,N,K)$, where $X=L$, and I. More generally, $f(I,L)=h(D,N,K)$. However, earning assets are only instruments that help the banking firm achieve its, sometimes alternative, ultimate financial goals: maximization of profits, total (net) earnings, or asset value for shareholders of the firm. Taking total earnings Y as the ultimate banking product for banking firms, there is a third-order transformation $Y=y(L,I,N,K)$. Therefore, the production of banking firms can be perceived as a multistage process: real resources are used to produce deposits; deposits are used to produce earning assets, which in turn are used to produce total earnings. The total earnings can therefore be expressed as a function of five categories of inputs: labor, capital, loans, investment, and deposits. The question is, how to organize these inputs in a banking firm production function?

The primary resources, such as labor and capital, play a different role in banking operations as compared to financial resources such as loans, investments, and deposits. The primary resources can be perceived as a medium or as operators via which the financial resources are organized and exchanged between banks and their customers. Bank operations involve a variety of decisions concerning banking resource allocation. Allocation decisions concerning certain resources may have different impacts on other resources. For example, a decision to increase personal loans will immediately affect the amount of

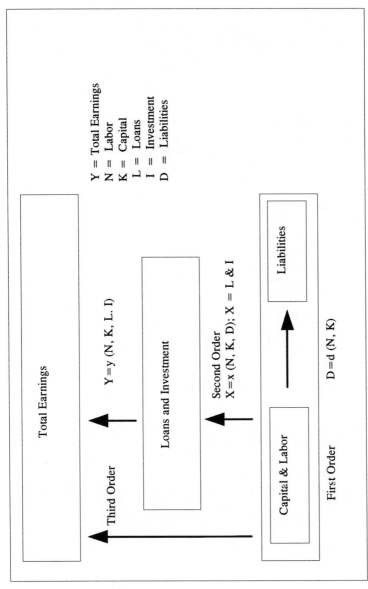

Figure 4.1 Three Levels of Transformation of Banking Activity

commercial loans and securities investments that a bank can issue. However, this adjustment can occur without any change in the amount of labor and capital used. Similarly, a reduction in transaction accounts may cause an immediate increase in nontransaction accounts when using the same amounts of labor and capital. The close mutual ties between various bank balance sheet items makes it crucially important to maintain healthy portfolios in all financial accounts, in order to increase asset values and reduce liability risks. Such portfolio managements generally have less immediate impact on labor and capital use than on financial resource use, except in a long-run banking expansion when both primary and financial resources change. Murphy and White (1983) pointed out that elasticity of substitution between labor and capital is likely to be greater than that between, for example, labor and deposits. The low immediate interaction between primary and financial resources indicates that primary resources and financial resources are profoundly different and therefore must be treated differently. In a separable production function, resources may be partitioned according to their elasticities of substitution. An example can be seen in the generalized Constant Elasticity of Substitution (CES) form, in which there exist within-group elasticities of substitution and between-group elasticities of substitution (Christensen *et al.* 1973). Following this logic, labor and capital, and financial resources can be grouped into two different partitions in a banking firm production function. Define

$$Y = F(L, I, D, N, K) = F\{g * f\} = F\{g(N, K) * f(L(D), I(D))\} \qquad (4.2)$$

where L and I can be seen as functions of D, while f is an aggregator function of L and I, describing the total output level without considering the level of labor and capital. Similarly, function, $g(N, K)$, is an index capturing the effect of labor and capital.

From the generalized function (4.2), three stages of transformation can be derived. Given any specific values Y_o, L_o, and I_o, shifting the right-hand side of (4.2) to the left results in:

$$Y_o - F_o\{g(N, K) * f(L_o(D), I_o(D))\} = 0 \qquad (4.3)$$

This is a function with respect to variables N, L, and D, while Y_o, L_o, and I_o act as parameters. Resolving the function for D leads to the first-order transformation. Considering D as an aggregator function of various deposits and liability items, a more general first-order transformation is $D(D_1, D_2, ...D_n) = g(L_1, L_2...L_i, I_1, I_2...I_j)$, where subscripts of D, L, and I depict different types of deposits, loans, and investment. In (4.3), let L and I be variables, leaving Y_o as a parameter. Resolving the function for L and I results in the second-order transformation. Again, a general form of the second-order transformation is $f(L_1, L_2, ...L_i; I_1, I_2, ...I_j) = g(N_1, N_2, ...N_w; K_1, K_2, ...K_r)$, where the subscripts of N and K indicate various labor and capital in the banking firm. In addition, equation (4.2) itself can be seen as a partial specification of the third-order transformation. A general form can be expressed as $Y = F(g*f)$, where $g = g(N_1, N_2, ...N_w; K_1, K_2, ...K_r)$ and $f = f(L_1(D_1..D_n), ..L_i(D_1, ..D_n), I_1(D_1, ..D_n), ..I_i(D_1, ..D_n))$.

Given the generalized banking firm production function (4.2), various functional specifications in the current literature discussed in Chapter III can be easily seen as special cases of the generalized form. For example, the first category banking output (total earnings or value added) is similar to describing banking behavior with the third-order transformation. The third category (dollar value of deposits) emphasizes the first-order transformation, taking other items as parameters. The second category uses the number of total banking accounts as a proxy of total earnings. This can be seen as a revised version of the first-order transformation. The fourth category basically (dollar value of earning assets) looks at the second-order transformation. The fifth category (dollar value of earning assets and deposits) simultaneously emphasizes the first- and second-order transformations. Thus, the generalized banking firm production function provides a consistent framework for analyzing banking activities.

Properties of the Function

Before turning to a multi-location extension of the above function, this section reveals some behavioral characteristics of the function constructed.

Weak Separability. Given that functions g and f are strongly separable in their respective components, function F is weakly separable in g and f. Proof is given as follows. Suppose $F = F\{g(N_1, N_2, K)*f\}$. Since

$$\partial Y/\partial N_1 = f\frac{\partial F}{\partial g}\frac{\partial g}{\partial N_1} \text{ and } \partial Y/\partial K = f\frac{\partial F}{\partial g}\frac{\partial g}{\partial K}$$

therefore

$$R_m = \frac{\partial Y}{\partial N_1}/\frac{\partial Y}{\partial K} = f\frac{\partial F}{\partial g}\frac{\partial g}{\partial N_1}/f\frac{\partial F}{\partial g}\frac{\partial g}{\partial K} = \frac{\partial g}{\partial N_1}/\frac{\partial g}{\partial K} \qquad (4.4)$$

Since $\partial g/\partial N_1$ and $\partial g/\partial K$ are functions of N_1, N_2, and K only, the marginal rate of substitution R_m is independent of f and its components L, I, and D. Thus, function F is weakly separable in f and g. Weak separability means that the banking firm optimizes the use of factors of production in separate groups. That is, the firm optimizes the combination of various labor and capital independent of the size of financial resources. In other words, for a given percentage change in input price, the elasticity of substitution between real resources (labor and capital) may be larger than those between real resources and financial resources, as revealed by Murphy and White (1983). This is much less restrictive than the conventional neoclassical functional form where uniform elasticities between all inputs are usually assumed.

Well-behaved Function. A well behaved nature for a function in the economic sense here refers mainly to continuity, twice differentiability, and diminishing marginal productivity. This requires the existence of the function and its first derivative function in its domain, positive first-order partial derivatives and negative second-order partial derivatives of the function with respect to various factors. The assumption of a well-behaved function becomes important in the next section where a multi-location profit-maximization banking firm's behavior patterns are sought. In order to obtain solutions to the series of optimum conditions given there, well-behaved functions are necessary and sufficient.

Suppose functions g and f are well-behaved. That is, $\partial g/\partial N > 0$, $\partial g/\partial K > 0$, $\partial^2 g/\partial N^2 < 0$, $\partial^2 g/\partial K^2 < 0$, $\partial^2 g/\partial N\partial K > 0$, $\partial f/\partial D = \partial f/\partial L\partial L/\partial D + \partial f/\partial I\partial I/\partial D > 0$, where $\partial f/\partial L > 0$, $\partial f/\partial I > 0$, $\partial L/\partial D > 0$, $\partial I/\partial D > 0$, and $\partial^2 f/\partial D < 0$. The conditions for $\partial^2 f/\partial D^2 < 0$ include $\partial^2 f/\partial L^2 < 0$, $\partial^2 f/\partial I^2 < 0$, $\partial^2 L/\partial D^2 < 0$, $\partial^2 I/\partial D^2 < 0$, and $0 < \partial^2 f/\partial L\partial I < \sigma$, where σ is a nonlinear combination of various derivatives and partial derivatives. A specification of σ is given in

Appendix A. Changing the right-hand side of (4.2) to the left of the equation results in an implicit function $G=Y-F=0$. Taking the total differential yields $G_Y dY + G_N dN + G_K dK + G_D dD = 0$. In this formula, G_X $(X=Y,N,K,D)$ are partial derivatives of G. $dK = dD = 0$, the partial derivative of Y with respect to N can then be obtained. A similar procedure can be used to obtain other partial derivatives. Thus,

$$\frac{\partial Y}{\partial N} = f \frac{\partial F}{\partial g} \frac{\partial g}{\partial N} > 0$$

$$\frac{\partial Y}{\partial K} = f \frac{\partial F}{\partial g} \frac{\partial g}{\partial K} > 0 \qquad (4.5)$$

$$\frac{\partial Y}{\partial D} = g \frac{\partial F}{\partial f} (\frac{\partial f}{\partial L} \frac{\partial L}{\partial D} + \frac{\partial f}{\partial I} \frac{\partial I}{\partial D}) > 0$$

Taking derivatives in each of the equations in (4.5) and collecting terms yields a set of negative second-order partial derivatives

$$\frac{\partial^2 F}{\partial N^2} = f(\frac{\partial^2 F}{\partial g^2} (\frac{\partial g}{\partial N})^2 + \frac{\partial F}{\partial g} \frac{\partial^2 g}{\partial N^2}) < 0$$

$$\frac{\partial^2 F}{\partial K^2} = f(\frac{\partial^2 F}{\partial g^2} (\frac{\partial g}{\partial K})^2 + \frac{\partial F}{\partial g} \frac{\partial^2 g}{\partial K^2}) < 0$$

$$\frac{\partial^2 F}{\partial D^2} = g[\frac{\partial^2 F}{\partial f^2} (\frac{\partial f}{\partial L} \frac{\partial L}{\partial D} + \frac{\partial f}{\partial I} \frac{\partial I}{\partial D})^2 \qquad (4.6)$$

$$+ \frac{\partial F}{\partial f} [\frac{\partial^2 f}{\partial L^2} (\frac{\partial L}{\partial D})^2 + \frac{\partial^2 f}{\partial I^2} (\frac{\partial I}{\partial D})^2$$

$$+ \frac{\partial f}{\partial L} \frac{\partial^2 L}{\partial D^2} + \frac{\partial f}{\partial I} \frac{\partial^2 I}{\partial D^2} + 2 \frac{\partial^2 f}{\partial L \partial I} \frac{\partial L}{\partial D} \frac{\partial I}{\partial D}]] < 0$$

When these conditions are met, it is easy to prove that the second-order condition for the function is met, since the function constructed includes two separable arguments g and f. This is a standard textbook well-behaved production function. The proof of the second-order condition can be found in any mathematical economics textbook.

Homothetic Function. It has been proved (Silberberg 1990) that a transformation of a homogeneous function results in a homothetic function. Assume functions g and f are homogeneous with degrees of homogeneity θ_g and θ_f respectively. Function $\xi = F(.) = g(N,K)*f(L,I)$ is therefore homogeneous of degree $\theta = \theta_g + \theta_f$. $F(.)$ means a transformation operation on a function homogeneous degree of $\theta = \theta_g + \theta_f$. It is therefore a homothetic function. In general, a homothetic function can be thought of as transferred from a linear homogeneous function by raising the linear homogenous function to the power defined by the degree of homogeneity. This means that the transformation $F(.)$ can be considered to include two steps. First is to transform ξ into a linear homogeneous function by taking the θ_ξth root of function ξ, i.e., $\xi^{1/\theta\xi}$. The second step is to transform the linear homogeneous function $\xi^{1/\theta\xi}$ into a homothetic function by raising the function to the θth power, i.e., $\xi^{\theta/\theta\xi}$. Thus, the homothetic function $F(g*f) = \xi^{\theta/\theta\xi} = (g*f)^{\theta/(\theta g + \theta f)}$. The essence of this transformation is to write a banking firm's production function into a linear homogeneous function with a degree of homogeneity. It thus separates the effect of scale from the effect of individual factors of production. This separation is important conceptually in that the degree of homogeneity is widely believed to be closely related to external agglomeration economies. Therefore it theoretically allows examination of the effect of the functional behavior itself, and the external environment separately.

Multi-location Banking Firm Production Functions

Arrow and Debreu (1954), and Debreu (1956) defined a commodity in three dimensions. These dimensions consist of a commodity's physical characteristics, its availability date, and its availability location. This is so because the same commodity offered at a different time and/or location has an entirely different economic meaning for a firm. Therefore, they are defined as different economic commodities. This definition of an economic commodity is an important and natural extension of the classical or textbook notion of market adjustment. The classical notion of market adjustment embodies the nature of point and instantaneity. That is, a commodity market exists at a point, or without friction (perfect mobility). Supply responds to change in demand instantaneously. Thus, time and space do not play a role in determining market price, leaving only one market for any commodity that is physically alike.[1] However, the introduction of time leads to the concept of discount. A commodity's value changes with time, resulting in the separation of the future market from the present market. Similarly, space will also change a commodity's value. This idea led Isard (1956) to suggest the concept of spatial discount when describing the change rate of commodity value with distance. Therefore, values may well be different at alternative locations for commodities that are physically alike.

The above definition of a commodity will directly influence the aggregation of a banking firm's production function. A multi-location banking firm uses different inputs according to their physical characteristics, time of availability, and location of availability. At one point in time, only location distinguishes inputs that are physically alike. A firm with two operating units each using three inputs is then treated as using six different inputs. The notion of substitution applies to all six inputs. As soon as the aggregation is carried out using such a principle, the derivation of a multi-location firm production function is straightforward.

Suppose the banking firm's facilities are located at three sites. At each site, the various inputs are aggregated in the way introduced in the previous section. Thus, the operation at each site can be expressed with a function $R_i = \xi_i^{\theta i}$, where $i = 1, 2, 3,$ and $\xi_i^{\theta i}$ are functions as defined in the previous section. That is, ξ is a linear homogeneous function, and θ is the degree of homogeneity. Indexing these three aggregate indices results in an higher level aggregate index $Y = F(R_1, R_2, R_3)$. This is the firm's production function with three plants. The key point here is that the operation at each site acts as a factor of production. The bank adjusts operations at various sites simultaneously. The optimum occurs when the expenditures on the last unit of operation at each site bring the same total earnings, an equilibrium condition for a profit-maximization banking firm, derived below.

This function can be easily extended to include more sites. It can also be extended to include operations of multi-class or multi-location at more aggregated levels. Suppose a bank holding company has operations in three classes of sites (for example, large, medium, and small metropolitan areas; or the East, South, and West). The total operation in each class of location is indexed as R_i, $i = 1, 2, 3$. The operation from three classes of locations constitutes the factors of production in production function $Y = F(R_1, R_2, R_3)$. In addition, suppose the banking industry in a region includes banks of three firm size classes. The industry acts as if an aggregate firm adjusts the operation of different size firms' operations. In this aggregate industrial level production function, each size class of firms constitutes a factor of production. Estimating this aggregate production function and comparing relevant parameters, such as the estimated marginal rate of substitution, may reveal whether the banking industry of the region is optimal, and what size class would need to increase its operation. This would provide the assessment of banking structure a direct efficiency criterion.

The function designed can prove to be compatible with the conventional and flexible functional forms. That is, the conventional and flexible functional specifications can be extended into multi-input, multi-output, multi-stage, and multi-location functions using the principles discussed previously. Here the conventional forms refer to the neoclassical Cobb-Douglas and Constant Elasticity of Substitution forms, and the flexible form refers to the transcendental logarithmic form (translog). Such compatibility with major functional specifications in production theory indicates that the multi-locational model designed is theoretically consistent with existing specifications. In other words, various existing specifications are only special cases of the function designed.

BANKING FIRM CONDUCT IN A SPATIAL CONTEXT

With a banking firm production function defined, banking conduct can be examined with more rigor. In this study, banking conduct means the mechanism or rules by which banking firms allocate their resources spatially or hierarchically in accordance with the external environment and internal objectives. The operational objective adopted in this research is maximization of profits. The external environment includes the externalities associated with economic conditions in which banks operate.

Suppose a profit-maximization banking firm operates at three locations. The multi-location production function is $Y = F(R_1, R_2, R_3)$, where R_i, $i = 1, 2, 3$, are indices for the three local operations. Each R is a homothetic function as defined in the previous section. That is, for each location, $R = (g*f)^\theta$, where $g*f$ is a linear homogeneous function. In the interests of brevity, subscripts have been omitted.

At the local level, local managers face the production function $R=(g*f)^\theta$, and cost function $C=w_L N+r_L K+t_L D$, where w_L, r_L, and t_L are local wage rates, rental rates on capital, and interest rates on deposits respectively. Thus, the objective function for the local manager is

$$\pi_i = R_i - C_i, \qquad i=1,2,3, \tag{4.7}$$

where π_i is profit at location i. The first-order conditions for profit maximization are

$$\frac{\partial \pi_i}{\partial N_i} = \frac{\partial R_i}{\partial g_i}\frac{\partial g_i}{\partial N_i}f_i - w_{Li} = 0,$$

$$\frac{\partial \pi_i}{\partial K_i} = \frac{\partial R_i}{\partial g_i}\frac{\partial g_i}{\partial K_i}f_i - r_{Li} = 0, \tag{4.8}$$

$$\frac{\partial \pi_i}{\partial D_i} = g_i\frac{\partial R_i}{\partial f_i}(\frac{\partial f_i}{\partial L_i}\frac{\partial L_i}{\partial D_i}+\frac{\partial f_i}{\partial I_i}\frac{\partial I_i}{\partial D_i}) - t_{Li} = 0$$

That is

$$\frac{\partial R_i}{\partial g_i}\frac{\partial g_i}{\partial N_i}f_i = w_{Li},$$

$$\frac{\partial R_i}{\partial g_i}\frac{\partial g_i}{\partial K_i}f_i = r_{Li}, \tag{4.9}$$

$$g_i\frac{\partial R_i}{\partial f_i}(\frac{\partial f_i}{\partial L_i}\frac{\partial L_i}{\partial D_i}+\frac{\partial f_i}{\partial I_i}\frac{\partial I_i}{\partial D_i}) = t_{Li}$$

Equations in (4.9) display standard neoclassical equilibrium conditions. That is, the marginal product value equals the factor price. Managers at the local level will adjust the resource at their disposal to make sure the above conditions are met. These conditions can be referred to as local equilibrium conditions.

At the firm level, executives face the production function $F(R_1,R_2,R_3)$ and cost function $C=\sum_i^3(w_i N_i+r_i K_i+t_i D_i)$, where w_i, r_i, and t_i are defined as before. An additional condition is that firm executives

are faced with output levels at various locations. That is, $R_i = R_i(.)$.
For banking firms as a whole, executives adjust output R among
various locations while local managers adjust inputs at particular
locations. The operation can be expressed with a Lagrangian function
with outputs at various locations as constraints. That is, a constrained
profit-maximization

$$L = F(R_1, R_2, R_3) - \sum_i^3 (w_i N_i + r_i K_i + t_i D_i) + \sum_i^3 \lambda_i (R_i - R_i(.)) \quad (4.10)$$

where λ_i are Lagrangian multipliers. The first-order conditions are

$$\frac{\partial L}{\partial R_i} = \frac{\partial F}{\partial R_i} - \lambda_i = 0$$

$$\frac{\partial L}{\partial N_i} = \frac{\partial F}{\partial N_i} - w_i - \lambda_i \frac{\partial R_i}{\partial N_i} = 0$$

$$\quad (4.11)$$

$$\frac{\partial L}{\partial K_i} = \frac{\partial F}{\partial K_i} - r_i - \lambda_i \frac{\partial R_i}{\partial K_i} = 0$$

$$\frac{\partial L}{\partial D_i} = \frac{\partial F}{\partial D_i} - t_i - \lambda_i \frac{\partial R_i}{\partial D_i} = 0$$

where $i = 1, 2$, and 3. For the second line, there is

$$\lambda_i = \frac{\dfrac{\partial F}{\partial N_i} - w_i}{\dfrac{\partial R_i}{\partial N_i}} = \frac{\dfrac{\partial F}{\partial N_i}}{\dfrac{\partial R_i}{\partial N_i}} - \frac{w_i}{\dfrac{\partial R_i}{\partial N_i}} \quad (4.12)$$

Assume the firm adjusts its operation at various locations so that the
marginal contribution to firm output from each location expansion is
equal. That is, marginal locational products λ_i are equal across the
locations. Therefore, for lines 2 and 3 in (4.11),

$$\lambda_i = \frac{\partial F / \partial N_i}{\partial R_i / \partial N_i} - \frac{w_i}{\partial R_i / \partial N_i} = \frac{\partial F / \partial K_j}{\partial R_j / \partial K_j} - \frac{r_j}{\partial R_j / \partial K_j} = \lambda_j \quad (4.13)$$

That is

$$\frac{\partial F/\partial N_i}{\partial R_i/\partial N_i} - \frac{\partial F/\partial K_j}{\partial R_j/\partial K_j} = \frac{w_i}{\partial R_i/\partial N_i} - \frac{r_j}{\partial R_j/\partial K_j} \qquad (4.14)$$

For the same location, i.e. $i=j$, the right-hand side of (4.14) is zero from the local equilibrium conditions (4.9). Thus

$$\frac{\partial F/\partial N_i}{\partial R_i/\partial N_i} - \frac{\partial F/\partial K_i}{\partial R_i/\partial K_i} = 0 \quad or \quad \frac{\partial F/\partial N_i}{\partial F/\partial K_i} = \frac{\partial R_i/\partial N_i}{\partial R_i/\partial K_i} \qquad (4.15)$$

Given that

$$\frac{\partial F}{\partial N_i} = \frac{\partial F}{\partial R_i}\frac{\partial R_i}{\partial N_i} = \frac{\partial F}{\partial R_i}\frac{\partial R_i}{\partial g_i}\frac{\partial g_i}{\partial N_i}f_i$$

and using the relationship in (4.9) and $\lambda_i = \lambda_i$, the conditions in (4.9) turn into local equilibrium conditions

$$\frac{(\partial F/\partial R_i)(\partial R_i/\partial N_i)}{(\partial F/\partial R_i)(\partial R_i/\partial K_i)} = \frac{\partial R_i/\partial N_i}{\partial R_i/\partial K_i} \qquad (4.16)$$

i.e.,

$$\frac{\partial R_i/\partial N_i}{\partial R_i/\partial K_i} = \frac{w_i}{r_i} \qquad (4.17)$$

For $i \neq j$, the right-hand side of (4.14) in equilibrium is also zero because $\lambda_i = \lambda_j$ in equilibrium. That is

$$\frac{(\partial F/\partial R_i)(\partial R_i/\partial N_i)}{\partial R_i/\partial N_i} - \frac{(\partial F/\partial R_j)(\partial R_j/\partial K_j)}{\partial R_j/\partial K_j} = \frac{w_i}{\partial R_i/\partial N_i} - \frac{r_j}{\partial R_j/\partial K_j}$$

$$(4.18)$$

or

$$0 = \lambda(\frac{\partial R_i/\partial N_i}{\partial R_i/\partial N_i} - \frac{\partial R_j/\partial K_j}{\partial R_j/\partial K_j}) = \frac{w_i}{\partial R_i/\partial N_i} - \frac{r_j}{\partial R_j/\partial K_j}$$

$$(4.19)$$

(4.14) becomes

$$\frac{\partial F/\partial N_i}{\partial R_i/\partial N_i} - \frac{\partial F/\partial K_j}{\partial R_j/\partial K_j} = 0$$

$$(4.20)$$

or

$$\frac{(\partial F/\partial R_i)(\partial R_i/\partial N_i)}{(\partial F/\partial R_j)(\partial R_j/\partial K_j)} = \frac{w_i}{r_j}$$

$$(4.21)$$

This is equivalent to

$$\frac{\partial F/\partial R_i}{\partial F/\partial R_j} = \frac{w_i/(\partial R_i/\partial N_i)}{r_j/(\partial R_j/\partial K_j)} = \frac{p_i}{p_j}$$

$$(4.22)$$

These are the equilibrium conditions for the allocation of assets among alternative locations. The left-hand side is the marginal rate of transformation. At the right-hand side, the numerator and denominator function as "cost" of locations i and j in that their magnitude determine the allocation of size R_i and R_j. A high "locational cost" requires a high marginal locational product and thus the size of assets at the location is reduced. Equilibrium is achieved when the marginal productivities of all locations are equal.

The "locational cost" term contains factor prices and the marginal productivity of factors at a particular location. Given that the local production function is $R = (g*f)^{\theta}$, the marginal product of a factor can be expressed as

$$\frac{\partial R_i}{\partial N_i} = \theta_i (g * F)^{(\theta_i - 1)} f_i \frac{\partial g_i}{\partial N_i} \qquad (4.23)$$

Substituting into (4.22) gives

$$\frac{\partial F/\partial R_i}{\partial F/\partial R_j} = \frac{\dfrac{w_i}{\theta_i (g_i * f_i)^{(\theta_i - 1)} f_i \dfrac{\partial g_i}{\partial N_i}}}{\dfrac{r_j}{\theta_j (g_j * f_j)^{(\theta_j - 1)} f_j \dfrac{\partial g_j}{\partial K_j}}} = \frac{p_i}{p_j} \qquad (4.24)$$

(4.24) reveals that the locational cost is positively related to the local price level, and negatively related to the marginal productivity of local factors, and the degree of homogeneity. A high local factor price will increase the locational cost p. A high locational cost requires the firm adjust the size of the local branch operation in order to obtain a high marginal locational productivity equal to the high locational cost. As a result, the size of the local branch operation is reduced.[2] On the other hand, a high marginal factor productivity in a local area, or a high level of externality associated with local economies such as urbanization and localization economies will reduce the locational cost p. Therefore, the marginal locational product will reduce and the size of the operation will increase. Specifically, the size of a branch is reversely related to factor prices but is directly related to the marginal factor productivity and the degree of homogeneity. In (4.24), $\partial g / \partial N$ acts as a shift term for function f, representing the magnitude by which an extra unit of input can affect the financial output f. Since $g*f$ is now defined as a linear homogeneous function, the partial derivative captures only the marginal factor productivity, and does not include the effects associated with various internal and external agglomerative economic factors.

The effects of various scale factors are captured by the degree of homogeneity, reflecting the economies that result from agglomeration of various economic factors. While some researchers (Shefer 1973) attribute the economies of scale captured by the degree of homogeneity for a firm level production function to the effect caused by agglomeration within a firm, and for a place level production function to external factors such as localization and urbanization economies, Carlino (1978) explained the returns to scale in a broader context including both internal and external agglomeration. That is, higher returns to scale may come not only from the fact that a firm benefits from large-scale production, but also because the firm is located in a place where positive externalities exist. Positive externalities include such things as favorable transportation, coordination conditions in various factor and commodity markets, and natural conditions including climate and water resources. This broader explanation of returns to scale captured by the degree of homogeneity indicates the possibility of decomposing returns to scale into various components associated with internal economies of scale and externalities associated with place conditions. Mathematically, this may be expressed with a place production function $R = (g*f)^{\alpha+\beta}$ where $\theta = \alpha + \beta$. Here α and β are reflections of internal and external agglomeration economies respectively. The place conditions can be seen as associated with various factors expressed in the conventional notion of localization and urbanization economies. These include the clustering of various producer services and corporate operations, and competitors in the banking industry as well. The results of competition and agglomeration may be reflected in factor prices available in particular local areas, and thus affect the branch size allocation.

Equation sets (4.11) contain 12 equations. Thus, the 12 unknown variables can theoretically be sought through resolving the equations simultaneously. These unknown variables are the sizes of operation at each of three sites, and their related levels of labor, capital, and deposits. The level of loans and investment are implicitly contained in the functions. Equations (4.9) and (4.11) describe a simultaneous adjustment process that may be understood as several separate optimum processes. At the local level, site managers adjust the level of labor L and capital K to obtain optimum g, and the level of deposits D (and hence the level of loans L and investment I) to obtain the optimum f. g and f the must be adjusted to obtain the optimum R. The optima R for different sites are then adjusted at the firm level to obtain the optimum total earnings Y.

MECHANISM OF AGGREGATE SPATIAL COMMUNITY BANKING OWNERSHIP AND OWNERSHIP NETWORK

Banking ownership across communities is the essential basis for multi-location banking through branch banking and interstate banking via bank holding. Such cross-community banking ownership forms what amounts to a corporate command/control network in the banking field. As discussed previously, studies in corporate geography in general, and banking geography in particular, suffer from a lack of theoretical rigor in that most theoretical arguments presented are inductive in nature. This forms a distinct contrast with the theoretical rigor of fields such as central place theory, and industrial and agricultural location theories. This section theoretically examines the mechanism by which the spatial banking ownership across communities is formed. The spatial banking network here is defined as the ownership network where banks in one community are owned by banks headquartered in other communities. The basic mechanism proposed is that the interaction between the utility function of a community and the production function of the other results in an equilibrium financial asset holding of the former community by the latter. Spatial networks of bank holding are seen as results of tradeoff between spatial interaction and non-spatial interaction in bank holding. In the following discussion, a scenario is first examined where a utility function and a production function interact to generate equilibrium cross-community banking assets holding. This is followed by a model in which communities' general utility functions are seen to contain their production functions. Thus a network of bank holding across communities can be derived. Both models can be readily transformed into a generalized gravity model. Therefore, these models provide a microeconomic foundation for the spatial interaction model.

The notion of "community" utility functions in this research is borrowed from neoclassical trade theory where countries are the unit of analyses (communities) and thus are assumed to demonstrate aggregate preferences in a commodity space. The concept of community in trade theory contains households and the business community defined by citizenship and nationality. In the context of this research, the concept of community refers to households and the business community in a locale such as a city or metropolitan area. For simplicity, assume that there is no multi-location residency among households and that no one owns multiple businesses that are headquartered in different communities. In addition, assume that conflicting interests within a community are negligible compared with common interests. These assumptions provide great convenience in analyzing economic interactions between communities.

The Model of Equilibrium Across Community Banking Ownership

Community Utility Function. Assume that there are two communities A and B. Community A has a utility function that contains a portfolio of items including financial assets and non-financial goods (such as goods and factors of production). The community adjusts the proportions of various items so that the utility can be maximized. Such a community utility function can be considered as a composite, separable function that exists as a result of aggregation of individual utility functions within the community. For convenience, all items are grouped into three major categories: D_O, deposits held by bank branches owned by community B but located in community A, D_I, deposits held by banks owned by community A and located in community A, and R, the rest of the items. This simplification can also be viewed in this way: assume an appropriate time span where only three items are variable and the rest of the items within the community are fixed. Thus, the maximization of utility can only be realized through adjustment of the three variable items. Specifically, the utility function is $U_A = U(D_I, D_O, R)$ where U_A is the utility of community A. The notion that a community can maximize its utility by allowing a certain amount of deposits to be held by another community is not without merit. A banking firm may actively search for an outside buyer in order to achieve a higher bid-price to maximize its asset value. Such a move would certainly increase the utility level for the community as a whole. External ownership cannot be considered negative as long as it remains at an optimal level.

The community would also incur certain costs for various items in the utility function. The cost for self-owned deposits is simply the interests on deposits i. Since depositors are not necessarily households and institutions from community A, this portion of payment constitutes a true cost to community A. The cost on the rest of the items R can be considered as an aggregate opportunity cost p, which consists of the benefits the community would otherwise enjoy under an alternative portfolio of items. The cost for externally owned deposits, t, is a function of interest on the deposits and the transaction cost. The transaction cost in this context can be understood as inconvenience and risk associated with external holdings. Such a transaction cost is likely to be a function of distance between community A and community B where the parent banks are located. This is so because increased distance between communities may result in imperfect information concerning the soundness of parent banks in the other community. The resulting poor judgment on the part of community A would increase its risk of being hurt financially when things go wrong in the other community. In addition, financial decisions on externally owned financial assets will be made outside of community A. There may be a lag in market change and decision-making, resulting in inconvenience. Given these conditions, the utility maximization problem in community A can be expressed as

$$\text{MAX } U_A = U(D_I, D_O, R)$$
$$\text{s.t. } V = Id_I + tD_O + Pr \qquad (4.25)$$

where V is the total budget of community A, or the total financial ability of the community during a certain time period such as one year.[3] From (4.25) a Lagrangian function is formed as

$$L = U + j(V - Id_I - Td_O - Pr) \qquad (4.26)$$

where j is a Lagrangian multiplier. The first-order conditions for maximization are

$$\frac{\partial L}{\partial D_I} = \frac{\partial U}{\partial D_I} - \lambda i = 0$$

$$\frac{\partial L}{\partial D_O} = \frac{\partial U}{\partial D_O} - \lambda t = 0 \qquad (4.27a)$$

$$\frac{\partial L}{\partial R} = \frac{\partial U}{\partial R} - \lambda p = 0$$

Given a locally competitive banking market where interest rates and other prices are out of the control of individual banks, the above set of equations contains three unknowns (D_I, D_O, and R). Solving the three equations can then provide the equilibrium values. From (4.27a)

$$\frac{\partial U/\partial D_I}{\partial U/\partial D_O}=\frac{i}{t} \qquad (4.27b)$$

This means that the utility can be improved through either internal bank owning or external bank owning. The equilibrium proportion will occur at the point where the rate of marginal utility substitution of the two types of bank owning is equal to their price ratio. This notion applies to other inputs as well.

In order to solve the equations, the utility function must be specified. Assume a Constant Elasticity of Transformation (CET) utility function

$$U_A=A(D_I^\theta+D_O^\theta+R^\theta)^{\frac{1}{\theta}} \qquad (4.28)$$

In the equation, θ is a substitution parameter. Substitute the utility function into (4.27a):

$$\frac{\partial L}{\partial D_I}=\frac{A}{\theta}(D_I^\theta+D_O^\theta+R_\theta)^{\frac{1}{\theta}-1}\theta D_I^{\theta-1}-\lambda i=0$$

$$\frac{\partial L}{\partial D_O}=\frac{A}{\theta}(D_I^\theta+D_O^\theta+R^\theta)^{\frac{1}{\theta}-1}\theta D_O^{\theta-1}-\lambda t=0 \qquad (4.29)$$

$$\frac{\partial L}{\partial R}=\frac{A}{\theta}(D_I^\theta+D_O^\theta+R^\theta)^{\frac{1}{\theta}-1}\theta R^{\theta-1}-\lambda p=0$$

i.e.,

$$\frac{\partial L}{\partial D_I}=\Delta D_I^{\theta-1}-\lambda i=0; \quad \frac{\partial L}{\partial D_O}=\Delta D_O^{\theta-1}-\lambda t=0; \quad \frac{\partial L}{\partial R}=\Delta R^{\theta-1}-\lambda p=0$$

$$(4.30)$$

where

$$\Delta=\frac{A}{\theta}(D_I^\theta+D_O^\theta+R^\theta)^{\frac{1}{\theta}-1}\theta \qquad (4.31)$$

Equation (4.30) can be solved as

$$D_O^{\theta-1} = \frac{t}{i} D_I^{\theta-1}; \quad D_I^{\theta-1} = \frac{i}{p} R^{\theta-1} \qquad (4.32)$$

Using the budget constraint in (4.25), (4.32) can be expressed as

$$D_O^{\theta-1} = \frac{t}{i} D_I^{\theta-1}$$

$$D_I^{\theta-1} = \frac{i}{p} \left[\frac{(V - iD_I - tD_O)}{p} \right]^{\theta-1} \qquad (4.33)$$

Solving (4.33) for D_I and D_O, and substituting results into the third line of (4.30) for R. The equilibrium solutions are found to be

$$D_I = \frac{V_A}{i^\mu (p^{-\mu\theta} + i^{-\mu\theta} + t^{-\mu\theta})}; \quad D_O = \frac{V_A}{t^\mu (p^{-\mu\theta} + i^{-\mu\theta} + t^{-\mu\theta})}; \quad R = \frac{V_A}{p^\mu (p^{-\mu\theta} + i^{-\mu\theta} + t^{-\mu\theta})}$$

$$(4.34)$$

where $\mu = (1-\theta)/\theta$, the elasticity of substitution. The above are demand functions for items D_I, D_O, and R. Demands for these items are positively correlated with the total budget, and negatively correlated with their own prices. However, these general relationships are mediated by other parameters in the system such as prices of other items, CET, and the elasticity parameter θ. The second line gives the equilibrium demand for external ownership. This amount is generally negatively correlated with the transaction cost and thus, negatively correlated with distance from parent banks. However, the existence of other parameters may blur the picture.

Community Banking Production Function. Assume that community B has a production function for its banking industry as a whole and that other factors of production are fixed. Therefore the only variable factors in the function are deposits held by banks owned by community B, and located in community B, d_I, deposits held by branches of community B but located in community A, d_O, and the remainder of the variable inputs L. The banking industry in community B also faces a total budget C. The price for d_I, I, is simply the interest paid on the internally owned deposits. The price for the rest of the variable inputs can be represented with a composite price P. The price for externally owned deposits is T. Again, this transaction cost contains interest paid on the externally owned deposits and inconvenience and risk associated with the spatial separation of the headquarters in community B and operating units in community A. Lack of information may cause lag of decision-making in adjusting to market changes in community A. In addition, the opportunity cost brought about by foregone benefits through owning deposits in alternative communities, contributes an additional element to the transaction cost. The banking industry in community B therefore can be expressed as

$$Q=Q(d_I,d_O,L)$$
$$\text{s.t.} \quad C=Id_I+Td_O+PL \tag{4.35}$$

where Q is the output of the banking industry in community B.
For a profit maximization problem MAX $\pi=Q\text{-}C$, the first-order conditions are

$$\partial\pi/\partial d_I=\partial Q/\partial d_I-I=0$$

$$\partial\pi/\partial d_O=\partial Q/\partial d_O-T=0 \tag{4.36a}$$

$$\partial\pi/\partial L=\partial Q/\partial L-P=0$$

From (4.36a), condition (4.36b) results in:

$$\frac{\partial Q/\partial d_I}{\partial Q/\partial d_O}=\frac{I}{T} \tag{4.36b}$$

This is also the equilibrium condition for alternative bank owning. Satisfaction of this condition will bring optimal levels of bank owning of all kinds.

Similarly, for a concrete solution, a Constant Elasticity of Substitution production function is introduced

$$Q=B(d_I^\sigma+d_O^\sigma+L^\sigma)^{\frac{1}{\sigma}} \tag{4.37}$$

where σ is an elasticity parameter, from which elasticity of substitution between factors can be calculated. Substituting the CES production function into (4.36) and using the budget constraint in (4.35), the solutions to equilibrium amounts of d_I, d_O, and L are

$$d_I = \frac{C_B}{I^\psi (P^{-\sigma\psi} + I^{-\sigma\psi} + T^{-\sigma\psi})}$$

$$d_O = \frac{C_B}{T^\psi (P^{-\sigma\psi} + I^{-\sigma\psi} + T^{-\sigma\psi})} \qquad (4.38)$$

$$L = \frac{C_B}{P^\psi (P^{-\sigma\psi} + I^{-\sigma\psi} + T^{-\sigma\psi})}$$

where $\psi = (1-\sigma)/\sigma$. The above gives the equilibrium amounts for the factors of production used in the banking industry. The second line represents deposits located in community A. For community A, this represents the supply of ownership on deposits located within A's territory. In a situation of spatial equilibrium, the amount required from A and supplied from B should be equal. Thus, $D_O = d_O$, that is

$$\frac{V_A}{t^\mu (p^{-\mu\theta} + i^{-\mu\theta} + t^{-\mu\theta})} = \frac{C_B}{T^\psi (P^{-\psi\sigma} + I^{-\psi\sigma} + T^{-\psi\sigma})} \qquad (4.39)$$

The relationship in (4.39) can be used to construct a generalized spatial interaction model. Define $D^2_{AB} = D_O d_O$, therefore

$$D_{AB} = \frac{V_A^{1/2} C_B^{1/2}}{t^{\mu/2} T^{\psi/2} (p^{-\mu\theta} + i^{-\mu\theta} + t^{-\mu\theta})^{1/2} (P^{-\psi\sigma} + I^{-\psi\sigma} + T^{-\psi\sigma})^{1/2}} \qquad (4.40)$$

Assume the budget for community A and the budget for the banking industry in community B are positively correlated with their capacity, expressed with community production functions $Q_A = Q(N_A, K_A)$ and $Q_B = Q(N_B, K_B)$ respectively, where N and K are labor and capital.

For a generalized Cobb-Douglas specification, (4.40) becomes

$$D_{AB} = \frac{(aN_A^{\alpha_A}K_A^{\beta_A})^{\epsilon_A/2}(bN_B^{\alpha_B}K_B^{\beta_B})^{\epsilon_B/2}}{t^{\mu/2}T^{\psi/2}(p^{-\mu\theta}+i^{-\mu\theta}+t^{-\mu\theta})^{1/2}(P^{-\psi\sigma}+I^{-\psi\sigma}+T^{-\psi\sigma})^{1/2}} \tag{4.41}$$

where a and b are parameters that establish the proportional relationships between budget and community production functions; α and β are output elasticities, and ϵ's are homothetic parameters. The above equation can also be written as

$$D_{AB} = \Delta \frac{N_A^{\underline{\alpha}_A}K_A^{\underline{\beta}_A}N_B^{\underline{\alpha}_B}K_B^{\underline{\beta}_B}}{T(d_{AB},i)} \tag{4.42}$$

where

$$\Delta = \frac{(ab)^{1/2}}{(p^{-\mu\theta}+i^{-\mu\theta}+t^{-\mu\theta})^{1/2}(P^{-\psi\sigma}+I^{-\psi\sigma}+T^{-\psi\sigma})^{1/2}}$$

$$\underline{\alpha}_A = \frac{\alpha_A\epsilon_A}{2}; \;\; \underline{\beta}_A = \frac{\beta_A\epsilon_A}{2}; \;\; \underline{\alpha}_B = \frac{\alpha_B\epsilon_B}{2}; \;\; and \;\; \underline{\beta}_B = \frac{\alpha_B\epsilon_B}{2} \tag{4.43}$$

$$T(d_{AB},i) = t^{\mu/2}T^{\psi/2}$$

and d_{AB} is the distance between communities A and B. For a CES functional specification, (4.40) becomes

$$D_{AB} = \Delta' \frac{(\alpha_A N_A^{\upsilon_A}+\beta_A K_A^{\upsilon_A})^{\epsilon_A/2\upsilon_A}(\alpha_B N_B^{\upsilon_B}+\beta_B K_B^{\upsilon_B})^{\epsilon_B/2\upsilon_B}}{T(d_{AB},i)} \tag{4.44}$$

where υ is an elasticity parameter.

If communities have stable labor-to-capital ratios, the amount of capital can be expressed by $K=kN$, where k is capital per unit of labor. The above equation becomes

$$D_{AB} = \Delta \frac{\left((\alpha_A + \beta_A k_A^{v_A}) N_A^{\mu_A}\right)^{\epsilon_A/2v_A} \left((\alpha_B + \beta_B k_B^{v_B}) N_B^{\mu_B}\right)^{\epsilon_B/2v_B}}{T(d_{AB}, i)} \qquad (4.45)$$

That is

$$D_{AB} = \Delta' \frac{N_A^{\epsilon_A/2} N_B^{\epsilon_B/2}}{T(d_{AB}, i)} \qquad (4.46)$$

where

$$\Delta' = (\alpha_A + \beta_A k_A^{v_A})^{\epsilon_A/2v_A} (\alpha_B + \beta_B k_B^{v_B})^{\epsilon_B/2v_B} \qquad (4.47)$$

The above derivation and resultant equations (4.40), (4.42), and (4.46), have provided an interpretation of the mechanism of spatial interaction slightly different from the conventional interpretation. The conventional interpretation of spatial interaction is that the degree of interaction is positively correlated with the size or attraction of places. The underlying rationale is that size and attraction are factors that affect volumes of demand and supply between places. The mechanism revealed above, first, sees spatial interaction as a resource allocation process in achieving maximization of utility or profits under budget constraint. For a local community both internal and external resources can be used to enhance utility or profit. Thus, there exists a substitution between spatial interaction (use of externally owned or located resources) and nonspatial interaction (use of internally owned or located resources). The equilibrium amount used from these two sources is determined where the marginal rate of substitution (4.27b) or the marginal rate of technological substitution (4.36b) between internal and external resources equal the ratio of resource prices. Under such conditions, an incremental investment in resources from different sources brings the same incremental utility or profit to the community.

Second, conditions in (4.27b) and (4.36b) rigorously describe the principle of comparative advantage. For example, a marginal rate of substitution between internal and external resources, less than their price ratio for a community, indicates lower marginal utility obtained by using internal resources. The community, therefore, has a comparative disadvantage in possessing resources. Seeking external owners would increase the community's utility. Clearly, spatial interaction can be seen to be based on the Heckscher-Ohlin neoclassical comparative advantage principle. In addition, (4.27b) and (4.36b) indicate that the price of an external resource is measured by transaction cost. Under the assumption that distance between communities plays a role in determining transaction cost, comparative advantage is consequently affected. For example, an increase in transaction cost associated with greater distance would reduce the price ratio in the previous example, resulting in a higher marginal rate of substitution. This indicates the existence of comparative advantage in internally owned resources. Thus, reduction of externally owned resources can increase utility. The principle of transferability is clearly shown.

Third, the size of community (whatever measure is used) is an indication of the size of supply and demand. However, a small community can also generate an unlimited volume of demand if there is no budget limitation. The size of supply and demand is financially determined by budget constraints. A high degree of interaction is a result of a high budget constraint. The existence of a budget constraint is the essential reason for efficient resource allocation. Thus, the concept of total budget seems to be more fundamental than size measures. The above derivation has shown that other measures of size can be conceptually seen as proxies for total community constraint. Equilibrium spatial resource allocation necessarily means that the marginal utility or marginal product from an extra unit of external ownership is the same everywhere. Given a banking field free of legal barriers, places with high budget constraints would be more likely to have high volumes of supply of external banking ownership that spread to a wide geographic area. Such external banking ownership closes the gap between communities in terms of marginal utility or productivity, resulting in spatial equilibrium.

The Model of Banking Ownership Network

Although the above case reveals the mechanisms of spatial interaction to a certain extent, the model derived is relatively simple in that there are only two communities included. In addition, one community has only a utility function and the other only a production function. More general models, which contain multiple communities and production and utility functions within the same community, can conceptually be developed by letting each community have a utility function, a banking industry production function, a community total budget constraint, and the banking industry budget constraint. In a maximization problem, the first function is the objective function, and the latter three are constraints. The asset holdings in each of the external communities can be specified as different factors in these functions. Such a system contains very many equations and increases the difficulty in mathematical manipulation and in reaching meaningful conclusions. As an alternative, the following is derived as a less rigorous version of the multi-community model.

Assume that each community has a utility function that contains financial resources, such as deposits. Among all deposits, some would be owned by the community itself, and others would be exchanged in ownership with other communities, either by selling out or buying in. For example, community A may sell ownership to community B, but would buy ownership from community C. An ownership portfolio thus exists. Such a function can be seen to describe a banking production function as a sub-component of the community utility function. The demand for owning external banking assets arises from the banking circle within a community. For simplicity, assume there is no mutual ownership. That is, if community A owns deposits in community B, B would not own deposits in A. Such an assumption is used not only to simplify the mathematical operation, but also has a strong real world basis. Chapter 5 of this book will show that mutual ownership of deposits among metropolitan areas is not important.

Specifically, suppose there are three communities A, B, and C. Community utility functions are as follows:

$$U_A = U(D_A^A, D_A^B, D_A^C, R_A)$$

$$U_B = U(D_B^A, D_B^B, D_B^C, R_B) \qquad (4.48)$$

$$U_C = U(D_C^A, D_C^B, D_C^C, R_C)$$

where D_j^i $(i=A,B,C; j=A,B,C)$ represents the deposits that the community j would want to exchange ownership with communities i, either to buy from i or to sell to i from j. When $i=j$, the deposits are owned by the community itself. R_j (j=A,B,C) is the rest of the variable assets of community j. The community budgets are given by

$$C_A = t_A^A D_A^A + t_A^B D_A^B + t_A^C D_A^C + p_A R_A \qquad (4.49.\text{i})$$

$$C_B = t_B^A D_B^A + t_B^B D_B^B + t_B^C D_B^C + p_B R_B \qquad (4.49.\text{ii})$$

$$C_C = t_C^A D_C^A + t_C^B D_C^B + t_C^C D_C^C + p_C R_C \qquad (4.49.\text{iii})$$

where t_j^i (i,j=A,B,C) is the transaction cost for ownership over D_j^i, when $i=j$, the transaction cost is reduced to the interest rate on the self-owned deposits, r_i (i=A,B,C), and p_i (i=A,B,C) is price for the rest of the variable items in the utility function.

For a particular community j, the first-order conditions for maximization of utility for a given budget constraint are given by

$$\frac{\partial L}{\partial D_j^i} = \frac{\partial U_j}{\partial D_j^i} - \lambda t_j^i = 0; \quad (i=A,B,C)$$

$$\frac{\partial L}{\partial R_j} = \frac{\partial U_j}{\partial R_j} - \lambda p_j = 0 \qquad (4.50)$$

where λ is a Lagrangian multiplier. Such a system of first-order conditions can also be transformed into forms similar to (4.27b) and (4.36b), indicating the conditions for equilibrium substitution between banking assets owning/holding in alternative communities. For a solution of the system, the CES utility function is introduced:

$$U_j = U(\sum_{i=A}^{B,C} (D_j^i)^{\theta_j} + R_j^{\theta_j})^{\frac{1}{\theta_j}} \qquad (4.51)$$

Using a similar procedure as previously discussed, the equilibrium amount of each item can be shown to be

$$D_j^i = \frac{C_j}{(t_j^i)^\mu (\sum_{i=A}^{B,C} (t_j^i)^{-\mu\theta} + p_j^{-\mu\theta})} \qquad (4.52)$$

For communities A, B, and C, there will be 3x4 equations as shown above. The focus here is on those equations that represent the ownership across communities. They are

$$D_A^B = \frac{C_A}{(t_A^B)^{\mu_A} \Delta_A} \qquad (i)$$

$$D_A^C = \frac{C_A}{(t_A^C)^{\mu_A} \Delta_A} \qquad (ii)$$

$$D_B^A = \frac{C_B}{(t_B^A)^{\mu_B} \Delta_B} \qquad (iii)$$

$$D_B^C = \frac{C_B}{(t_B^C)^{\mu_B} \Delta_B} \qquad (iv)$$

$$(4.53)$$

$$D_C^A = \frac{C_C}{(t_C^A)^{\mu_C} \Delta_C} \qquad (v)$$

$$D_C^B = \frac{C_C}{(t_C^B)^{\mu_C} \Delta_C} \qquad (vi)$$

$$where \quad \Delta_j = (\sum_{i=A}^{B,C} (t_j^i)^{-\mu_j \beta_j}) + (p_j)^{-\mu_j \beta_j}$$

$$j = A, B, C$$

where

$$\Delta_j = (\sum_{i=A}^{B,C} (t_j^i)^{-\mu_j \theta_j}) + (p_j)^{-\mu_j \theta_j}$$

$$j = A, B, C$$

General equilibrium requires

$$D_A^B = D_B^A, D_A^C = D_C^A, \text{and } D_B^C = D_C^B \qquad (4.54)$$

Using the methodological steps previously described, the three interaction equations are revealed to be

$$D_{AC} = \frac{(C_A)^{1/2}(C_C^{1/2})}{(t_A^C t_C^A)^{1/2}(\Delta_A \Delta_C)^{1/2}} \qquad (4.55a)$$

$$D_{AB} = \frac{(C_A)^{1/2}(C_B^{1/2})}{(t_A^B t_B^A)^{1/2}(\Delta_A \Delta_B)^{1/2}} \qquad (4.55b)$$

$$D_{BC} = \frac{(C_B)^{1/2}(C_C^{1/2})}{(t_B^C t_C^B)^{1/2}(\Delta_B \Delta_C)^{1/2}} \qquad (4.55c)$$

Substituting production functions into the above equations, writing the transaction cost as functions explicitly containing the distance argument, and combining constant terms into a single constant, gives

$$D_{AC} = \Delta_{AC} \frac{(f_A)^{\epsilon_A/2}(f_C)^{\epsilon_C/2}}{T_{AC}(d_{AC}, r_A, r_C)} \qquad (4.56a)$$

$$D_{AB} = \Delta_{AB} \frac{(f_A)^{\epsilon_A/2}(f_B)^{\epsilon_B/2}}{T_{AB}(d_{AB}, r_A, r_B)} \qquad (4.56b)$$

$$D_{BC} = \Delta_{BC} \frac{(f_B)^{\epsilon_B/2}(f_C)^{\epsilon_C/2}}{T_{BC}(d_{BC}, r_B, r_C)} \qquad (4.56c)$$

where f_i's ($i = A, B, C$) are production functions, and ϵ's are homothetic parameters.

Equations (4.56a) to (4.56c) describe a system of spatial interaction or a place network through spatial interaction, specifically through deposit ownership among communities. This network can be succinctly described by

$$D(D_{AB}, D_{AC}, D_{BC}) = F(f_A, f_B, f_C, T(d_{AB}, d_{AC}, d_{BC}, r_A, r_B, r_C)) \qquad (4.57)$$

Function $D(D_{AB}, D_{AC}, D_{BC})$ describes all inter-community deposit ownerships. Function $F(.)$ illustrates factors that can be used to predict the magnitude of these spatial flows of deposit ownership. Consider banking firms in the three communities as one banking industry and write $D(.)$ as a CES form

$$D = (D_{AB}^\zeta + D_{AC}^\zeta + D_{BC}^\zeta)^{\frac{1}{\zeta}} \qquad (4.58)$$

This formula clearly shows the possible substitution among different flows. In other words, flows may occur between alternative community pairs. Flow patterns occur due to individual community utility maximization motivation. As shown in (4.48) to (4.50), allocation of flows may occur among alternative communities. Different destinations are weighed according to the incremental utility that an incremental flow can bring to the community. Equilibrium flow patterns occur where the incremental increase in flow between any community pair brings the same incremental increase in utility to the community. Such a mechanism is equivalent to the rationale given in the principle of competing destinations.

For the banking industry as a whole, aggregate equilibrium flow patterns are the result of the equilibrium flows of each community pair. Industry performance efficiency partly depends on such flow of ownership. As pointed out previously, nonspatial interaction and spatial interaction can be seen as reflecting the alternative means for a local community to maximize their utility. With lack of market power, such free spatial movement of corporate ownership across communities reflects resource allocation based on comparative advantage determined by the price ratio available at different communities. Allowing free movement of resource ownership based on comparative advantage results in agreement between the marginal rate of substitution of resources and the price ratio. This brings maximization of utility to local communities and efficiency to the banking industry. When market power exists, however, monopolistic prices result. The price ratios are therefore distorted, not reflecting locational comparative advantage. Many states refuse big money center banks entry through mergers and acquisition, partly reflecting local concern over their own interest or utility. The study of banking concentration provides a channel to monitor market competitiveness. However, for the entire U.S. banking industry, perhaps, more a important issue is whether or not banks should have more freedom to interact spatially rather than limiting spatial movement of corporate ownership. The weak federal legislation concerning branch banking, results in a situation in which state lines become branch expansion market boundaries. Recent state initiatives on interstate banking legislation have helped the creation of regional interstate banking pacts, at least legally, bringing down spatial barriers for states in geographical proximity but establishing spatial barriers to remote states. In light of the banking spatial mechanism discussed above, these barriers are detrimental to the entire banking industry although the local community utility may benefit.

CONCLUSIONS

The above analyses of banking firm conduct treat the spatial behavior of a banking firm as allocating size of branch operations among alternative locations. According to this size allocation model, the firm adjusts the sizes for a spectrum of branch operations to achieve profit maximization. To produce a given level of banking output, different branch size combinations are possible. The optimal branch size combination occurs where the total cost is a minimum. The equilibrium condition occurs when the marginal rate of transformation equals the ratio of locational costs. This model suggests several important characteristics concerning the spatial behavior of banking firms.

The first concerns the factors determining banking firm spatial expansion. One factor concerns resource costs in targeted areas. Low resource costs generally encourage entry to new markets or expansion in existing markets. Another factor is externalities of the branch locations. A positive externality also encourages expansion of banking firms. As discussed previously, these positive externalities may be a combination of many factors available in a locale, and their aggregate effects on banking are usually described by urbanization and localization economies. This explains the attraction of large metropolitan areas as banking fields. In addition, the productivity of banking firms in a local area also affects their spatial expansion. Firms tend to expand to those areas where they can operate under high productivity. When there exist economies of scale that can increase productivity, large banks have the advantage to expand.

The second characteristic of the spatial behavior of a banking firm is that the firm seeks equilibrium in its entire operating network. The spectrum of branch locations forms a operating network for the firm. The relative importance of each site is affected by conditions available at all sites. In other words, relative sizes of all locations in a network are determined simultaneously. A local manager may seek aggressive expansion at a location to obtain location profit maximization. Such a move may be weighed and balanced by the firm executives to obtain optimization at the firm level. There exists substitutability among alternative sites. For a given output and input combination, the elasticities of substitution among alternative sites indicate the relative importance of each site. Thus, important banking centers and markets are likely to have small elasticities of substitution. That is, for a banking firm, important banking centers are less substitutable than less prominent centers.

The third characteristic of banking firm operation in a spatial context is that the location issue is only one of the resource allocation issues that must be considered. In addition to the decision concerning the optimal location/size mix (in other words, a network and relative importance of each site in the network), a firm is faced with many other important allocation decisions such as optimal output and input mixes. The interaction between location/size decisions and other decisions jointly determines network patterns. For a given mix of outputs and inputs, an optimal location/size mix can be determined. When output mix and input mix vary, the location/size mix changes too. Among all possible combinations of location/size mix, output mix, and input mix, the firm will choose the one that provides the maximum profit or the minimum cost. This simultaneous decision-making process has at least two implications concerning the nature of banking networks. First, due to the subjective nature of preferences of individual firms, output mix and input mix (in other words, production space or preference space) are unlikely to be identical between two banking firms. Thus, the existence of identical firm networks is theoretically unlikely. Second, the elasticities of substitution between inputs that are located in different locations may have various magnitudes, depending upon, among other things, the nature of the ownership of the banking firm. These magnitudes may be large for a branch system but small for a bank holding company system. Thus, the magnitudes of substitution may reflect the integrity and coherence of a network.

The analyses of macro-level banking conduct have revealed a mechanism for the spatial division of labor within the banking industry. That is, across community banking ownership is seen as equilibrium bank holding in achieving community utility maximization. The substitutions between spatial interaction and nonspatial interaction, and between different community pairs are the result of two factors. The first is that different kinds of banking holdings are associated with different utility improvements. The second concerns the cost associated with different kinds of holdings. For given costs, powerful banking communities, with wide existing business connections and rich market information, may be able to achieve high utility through external banking ownership in multiple communities and thus become command/control centers in corporate banking networks. For a given banking industry, lowering costs between communities will encourage external ownership. An example is seen in the U.S. banking industry, in which change in transaction cost is reflected in reduced limitations on geographic restrictions on banking, and resultant changes in the corporate banking landscape. When considering both factors mentioned above, different scenarios may occur concerning interstate banking strategy. Banking communities with strong ability to increase their utility through external ownership would want to lower barriers to interstate banking. Banking communities with rising power may maintain certain transaction costs to powerful out-of-state banks by imposing limitations (such as regional and/or reciprocal) on interstate banking in order to protect their own banking industry. In addition, communities with a weak banking industry may lower transaction costs to out-of-state banks in order to attract banking capital and raise asset values. All these different strategies are designed to protect community interests and improve community welfare. Place networks are therefore formed as a result of economic interest on the one hand, and political power structure as reflected in banking regulations on the other. For a country like the United States where the enormous physical extent of the country encompasses a great diversity in terms of level of development, and a unique historical background has helped form a highly decentralized political structure and related banking regulatory system, the aggregate place banking networks would necessarily exhibit strong impressions of these two elements.

The spatial behavior of banking firms and the banking industry as revealed in this chapter may have a variety of consequences in an economy. Two particular aspects are within the scope of this research. These are banking firm performance and the aggregate place banking network structure, which are the subjects of the next two chapters.

NOTES

1. It would be inappropriate to conclude that the classical notion of market adjustment is totally wrong. Classical theory provides a starting point from which later work extends the market adjustment notion into more realistic situation by relaxing prescribed assumptions in classical models.

2. This is so because of the well-behaved nature of the production function constructed. A well-behaved function has positive first-order derivatives and negative second-order derivatives with respect to the factors of production. Thus, the marginal productivity is a downward sloping curve. Equilibrium requires equalization of the marginal productivity and locational cost. Given a higher locational cost, a higher marginal productivity is obtained by reducing the size of branch operation.

3. The total community budget here is equivalent to the total household income in the context of a household utility function. This consists of the amount of resources or wealth available for a community on a yearly basis in order to pay for the items in the utility function.

V

Spatial and Hierarchical Structures of Corporate Banking Ownership in the U.S. Metropolitan System

This chapter addresses the second research question, which concerns the geographic structure of banking corporate ownership and dominance in the U.S. metropolitan system. This is an empirical investigation of the spatial and hierarchical structure of banking corporate networks under branch and bank holding company ownership in the U.S. metropolitan landscape. In addition, attention is given to the dominance of the largest metropolitan areas in the banking field.

The first section discusses the data and methods used in constructing metropolitan banking corporate networks. Section 2 presents the landscape of branching bank networks, and is followed by section 3 in which the landscape of bank holding networks and patterns of interstate banking are presented. The dominance of the largest metropolitan areas in the banking field is discussed in section 4. Section 5 illustrates the latest developments in interstate banking. The last section gives a brief summary of the findings.

DATA AND METHODOLOGY
IN BANKING NETWORK ANALYSES

The spatial structure of the banking corporate network in this study is defined as the interconnection formed through banking ownership among metropolises. Such connections between metropolitan areas not only provide ties between metropolises, but also form dominance command/control hierarchical structures within a certain geographic territory. A fundamental task in analysis of the spatial structure of banking corporate networks, as defined in this dissertation, is to identify their hierarchical structure and geographic extent. This requires identifying the magnitude of banking assets of banking institutions (head offices and/or branch offices) located in a place that are owned by banking institutions located in the place itself and in all other places. In other words, a place ownership portfolio for the total financial assets of all banking offices located in a place must be established.

For example, as of 1991, there were 41 banking offices (including both head and branch offices) operating within the boundary of metropolitan Athens, Georgia. The total withdrawable deposits of these offices was 913 million dollars. Among these offices and deposits, 34 offices and 615 million dollars are owned by banks headquartered in Athens, and 7 offices and 298 million dollars are owned by banks headquartered in other metropolitan areas. Banks in Atlanta owned 5 offices and 84 million dollars, and banks in Savannah owned 2 offices and 214 million dollars. Place portfolios can also be constructed for higher order ownership such as bank holding companies. For example, 19 offices or 756 million dollars of deposits in Athens are owned by bank holding companies headquartered in Atlanta (9 offices and 309 million dollars) and Norfolk, Virginia (5 offices and 214 million dollars). However, banks headquartered in Athens had no branch offices in other metropolitan areas. The only holdings outside Athens involved 4 branch offices and 68 million dollars worth of deposits in nonmetropolitan areas. In addition, no bank holding companies were headquartered in Athens. Such place ownership portfolios provide a clear indication of Athens' position in terms of dominance and command/control in the entire metropolitan banking system. In order to establish the banking corporate command/control structure and dominance hierarchical field within the metropolitan system, place ownership portfolios must be constructed for all metropolises, and the geographical and hierarchical relationships among metropolises analyzed.

To accomplish this task, this study uses the magnetic tape *Summary of Deposits for All FDIC-insured Depository Institutions for 1991* (the *Deposits tape*). This tape contains deposit information for all commercial and saving banks in the U.S and its territories. For each bank, the tape separately lists summary information for the bank as a whole and information on its head office and branch offices. The head office here refers to the operating unit that has the same location as the headquarters. For example, the Trust Company Bank of Athens has its headquarters at 101 North Lumpkin Street, Athens. The same location houses one of its operating units. This particular operating unit is defined here as the head office. A branch office is defined by the FDIC as banking offices providing full services, taking deposits, or granting loans (Golembe and Holland 1986). Although the court has ruled that Automatic Teller Machines (ATMs) are branches, the *Deposits tape* contains information on only brick and mortar branches. Thus ATMs are not included in the present study. Information for head and branch offices includes the location (street address, city, county, metropolitan area, state or territory) of the offices and the amount of deposits in those offices. Such information makes it possible to trace the geographical spread of operational networks for any bank. Aggregating such locational networks for all banks headquartered in a metropolitan area generates a geographic field which contains operating units headquartered in that metropolitan area. The same procedure is applied to other metropolitan areas to obtain operating units located in the metropolitan area in question but headquartered in other metropolitan areas. Thus, a place portfolio is established for the metropolitan area. Application of this procedure to the entire metropolitan system will generate a place network where interrelationships between metropolitan areas are expressed as cross metropolitan banking ownership in terms of the number of offices and the amount of deposits.

Two types of banking ownership are separately identified: branching ownership and ownership based on bank holding companies. Thus, two separate place networks are constructed. These separate place networks are used as the basis for analyzing and comparing bank corporate landscapes based on branch and bank holding ownerships. Identification of bank holding company place networks is also based on the *Deposits tape* but additional bank holding company codes must be extracted from a separate magnetic tape, *Income and Financial Statement for All Banks* (the *Income tape*). The *Income tape* contains consolidated balance sheet and income statements for all commercial and saving banks in the United States. Although no information on individual operating units is given, the *Income tape* contains bank holding company codes that identify banks belonging to the same bank holding company. Linking these bank holding company codes to banks and their operating units in the *Deposits tape* allows identification of locations of operating units that belong to the same bank holding companies. The place network based on bank holding ownership can then be constructed.

Since this study focuses on the metropolitan system, only those banks that are headquartered in metropolitan areas are included in the data set. In addition, bank operating units that are either headquartered or located in U.S. territories are not included in the data set. Foreign banks in the United States can be grouped into individuals and banking organizations that owned or invested in U.S. banks and those that operate agencies. The former can take deposits and enjoy bank insurance as do domestically owned banks. These banks are included in the *Deposits tape* and therefore included in the analysis. No effort is made to distinguish them from domestically owned banks since the purpose of this research is to identify the corporate and operational ownership rather than the nationality of the ownership. Foreign agencies are not allowed to take deposits, therefore, their activities are not reflected in the *Deposits tape* though the *Income tape* contains consolidated financial information. Since this information is not location-specific, it is not helpful in construction of a place network. This group of foreign banks is not included in this study. Branches of foreign banks are also excluded from the analysis, since one of the primary purposes of this study is to trace the command/control relationships between places associated with banking corporate ownership in the U.S. metropolitan system. Branches of foreign banks are headquartered in foreign countries. A thorough analysis of command/control relationships associated with foreign banks requires a worldwide scope. Such a scope is beyond the purpose of this study.

In order to obtain information that is as consistent as possible from the two tapes, the June 31, 1991 issues of both the *Deposits tape* and *Income tape* were used. Since these tapes are reported quarterly, the June 31 issues reflect the situation up to the second quarter of 1991. The *Deposits tape* contains 335 metropolitan areas as defined in 1990. Within these metropolitan areas, 5,504 banks and 612 bank holding companies are located. Therefore, the metropolitan banking corporate networks will be constructed among these banking institutions and places. In summary, a 335-by-335 place ownership matrix, or matrix of spatial banking ownership flow, is constructed for the branch system. Another matrix is constructed for the bank holding system.

Since the flows between places are frequently used in this research, some relevant definitions must be provided as follows. Outflow ownership refers to the amount of banking assets that a place owns but which are located outside that place. Inflow ownership refers to that portion of banking assets in a place that are owned by banks headquartered outside that place. Inflow and out-flow are items that are extractable from a flow matrix. On-site ownership refers to that portion of the total banking assets of a place that are owned by banks headquartered in that place.

In analyzing the matrix of banking ownership flow, the principles of dominant-flow proposed by Nystuen and Dacey (1961) are used. This approach constructs hierarchical relationships between places using two criteria: the order of places and the dominant flow (maximum flow) between places. The order of places determines the relative dominance between places, while the magnitude of flow indicates the closeness between places. For a given order of places, the hierarchical relationships between places are determined by the following three principles (Nystuen and Dacey 1961; Taaffe and Gauthier 1973):

Principle One, a city is independent if its largest flow is to a smaller city; and a city is subordinate if its largest flow is to a larger city.

Principle Two, if city A is subordinate to city B, and city B is subordinate to city C, then city A is subordinate to city C. As a result, this principle is called "Transitivity."

Principle Three, a city cannot be subordinate to any of its subordinates.

This approach provides the important principles needed to sort out internal structure from a raw flow matrix and has been widely used in various flow analyses (Nystuen and Dacey 1961; Miyagi 1969; Taaffe and Gauthier 1973; Wheeler and Mitchelson 1989). This research adopts this dominant-flow analysis approach with certain revisions.

The first revision relates to the particular flow patterns in the banking ownership matrix. In most previous flow analyses (Nystuen and Dacey 1961; Wheeler and Mitchelson 1989), the flows occur in both directions between any two places. This is revealed by a matrix with very few empty cells and thus high density.[1] The resultant hierarchical structure usually contains most of the places in the system. In other words, the digraph[2] is more likely to be minimally connected. Banking ownership between places in the United States, however, consists in most cases, of one way flows. In addition, state branch banking regulations may severely reduce the chance for flows between places. Consequently, the banking ownership flow matrix contains a large number of empty cells and has a low density. Larger centers especially may have a greater chance to have banking ownership in smaller centers while smaller centers have very little chance to own banking facilities in larger centers. The resultant hierarchical digraph based on Principle One is likely to be disconnected. In other words, there will be many independent centers. In order to link as many independent centers as possible to the hierarchical structure, an additional fourth principle is proposed as follows.

Principle Four, a lower order independent center will be subordinated to a higher order center that has the maximum out-flow of banking ownership into it. In this research, this maximum out-flow is global. That is, the maximum in a column.

Conceptually, Principle Four can be seen as an extra step in organizing hierarchical flow structure, i.e., Principle One is used to distinguish independent centers from dependent centers. After various independent centers are identified using Principle One, Principle Four is used to define the relationships between various independent systems. Principles Two and Three are still applied.

Another revision of the dominant-flow analysis relates to the determination of the order of places. Since it is one of the criteria used in analyzing the hierarchical structure, determination of the order of places is crucial. Both Nystuen and Dacey (1961), and Taaffe and Gauthier (1973) used the within-approach to determine the order of centers. Specifically, the magnitude of the cumulative flow into a place (column sum) was used to classify places' orders. Nystuen and Dacey's work focused on telephone call flows between city pairs. In any city pair, a larger city is more likely to receive more phone calls than does the smaller city. Thus, the in-flow approach is intuitively understandable. However, in banking ownership flow, smaller places are less likely to generate major out-flow of ownership into larger places than the other way around. In light of the command/control function, a larger in-flow of ownership is more likely to be an indication of magnitude of being controlled (Wheeler 1988), although at the same time it may also indicate the size of the available assets. Complicating this ambiguity is the intuition that more important centers are likely to possess more external resources (Wheeler 1988; Lord 1992). This intuition supports the use of cumulative out-flow of ownership to classify the order of places. In order to avoid such ambiguity, this research adopts an outside-approach to determine the order of places. Specifically, the sum of the cumulative inflow and out-flow, and on-site ownerships is used to classify the order of places. Here on-site ownership is obtainable only from outside the flow matrix. The advantage of this criterion is that it encompasses several components. Ambiguity in one element can be offset by clear definitions in other elements. Thus, results are less biased. For example, ambiguity concerning a place's order as a result of a large cumulative inflow ownership is reduced if it is known that the place also possesses substantial on-site and external ownerships. This additional information helps rank and distinguish places with similar amounts of inflow ownership.

SPATIAL AND HIERARCHICAL STRUCTURES OF CORPORATE BANKING UNDER THE BRANCH BANKING SYSTEM

Study of the geographical structure of banking corporate ownership under a branching network consists of three related components: the state metropolitan banking spatial structure, the state metropolitan banking hierarchical structure, and the relationships between the banking spatial structure and hierarchical structure.

Spatial Structure of Metropolitan Systems Under the Branch Banking Network

National Level: High Fragmentation. The current status of state branch banking legislation is a reliable indication of the possible spatial structure of banking corporate ownership under branching networks. Independent state branch bank laws have kept state branch banking systems in isolation, resulting in high fragmentation at the national level. The first indication of fragmentation is that the 335-by-335 banking ownership flow matrix has numerous empty cells and thus has an extremely low density. The total number of possible entries across metropolitan areas is $N(N-1)=111,890$, where N is the number of metropolitan areas in the system. The actual number of entries is 772, which gives a density of 0.0069.

Another indication of fragmentation is that the great majority of ownership is on-site in nature. The total number of banking offices, including both head and branch offices, owned by banks headquartered in the metropolitan system is 45,409. Among them, 4,736 or 10.4% are located in nonmetropolitan areas; 28,585 or 63.0% are located within their own metropolitan areas; 12,088 or 26.6% exhibit cross metropolitan ownership. In terms of the amount of deposits, of the total withdrawable deposits of 2,133,486.8 million dollars owned by metropolitan banks, 122,257.4 million dollars or 5.7% are located in nonmetropolitan areas; 1,538,408.8 million dollars or 72.1% have on-site ownership; less than a quarter, 472,820.6 million dollars, or 22.2% have cross metropolitan ownership. The low percentage of external ownership indicates the generally weak ties between places compared with the strong inward tendency, as evidenced by the high percentage of on-site ownership. A closer examination shows that the most important factor that contributes to the spatial fragmentation of the banking industry is the lack of cross metropolitan ownership between different states. The overwhelming number of entries occur among metropolitan areas within the same state with only two exceptions. The first exception occurs within those metropolitan areas that cross state lines. The second exception is seen in a few cases of true interstate branching as discussed in Chapter II. The total possible number of intra-state cross metropolitan ownerships is 3,796. With 772 intra-state cross metropolitan entries, the overall intra-state density is 0.2034. The number of possible interstate cross metropolitan ownership entries is 108,094. None of the cells are filled. Essentially, each state branching system exists in isolation. There are literally 50 state branch networks in operation.

Spatial Variations. Although state branch banking legislation cuts the U.S. branch banking corporate network into 50 separate segments, wide structural variations can be found between these 50 systems. A cluster analysis is conducted over the first three principal components of eight structural variables: percentages of out-flow, on-site, and nonmetropolitan ownerships, plus percentages of unit banking offices and deposits.[3] In deciding the number of clusters, there is often a lack of any objective standard since the minimum distance between clusters may increase gradually when the number of groups reduces. This was the case in this research. This research adopts a grouping based on two principles. First, the number of groups must be at a manageable level; and second, no single state forms a cluster, a necessary condition in order to obtain sufficient number of banks in each cluster to conduct statistical estimation in Chapter VI. Although minor variations in groupings exist when various different clustering methods are applied, the general tendency is clear. The most consistent grouping is obtained using the Ward minimum variance approach. Seven clusters result. To explicitly reveal characteristics of these clusters, the average structural percentages and standard deviations are calculated for each cluster (Tables 5.1 and 5.2). Using these averages and the U.S. metropolitan system average, structural quotients are calculated and are presented in Table 5.3. Based on the magnitude of the structural quotients, these seven clusters can be characterized in terms of their structural orientation. Figure 5.1 shows the geographic distribution of the seven clusters of structural orientation. The following is a brief description of these clusters.

Cluster I, Mainstream Structural Orientation. In many ways, this cluster represents the general structure for the U.S. metropolitan system as a whole. With the exception of unit banks, structural percentages in this cluster do not significantly differ from U.S. metropolitan averages (When the t test is conducted, the null hypothesis fails to be rejected at the 0.975 level for out-flow, at the 0.95 level for on-site, and at the 0.75 level for nonmetropolitan ownerships). This similarity is reflected in structural quotients close to one in the three major structural categories, and exists because many systems in this cluster are large in terms of the size of the economy and therefore the banking industry. Examples are New York, Florida, Texas, Pennsylvania, Ohio, Michigan, Massachusetts, and to a certain extent, Georgia, Tennessee, Washington. This can be seen from their categorical shares in the national metropolitan total. Seven of the top ten largest deposit states are in this cluster (Figure 5.2). Five of the top ten in terms of largest nonmetropolitan ownership by absolute amount are in this cluster (Figure 5.3). In addition, seven out of the top ten largest in on-site and five of the top ten in out-flow ownership measured by the absolute amounts are in this cluster (Figure 5.4 and Figure 5.5). As a result, metropolitan banking structures in these states are highly influential in shaping the U.S. metropolitan banking structure as a whole. It is also important to recognize that in most states in this cluster, statewide branching is legal (Figure 5.6). The presence of large out-flow deposits

Table 5.1 Cluster Structure Based on Amount of Deposits*

Cluster	State	Out-Flow	On-Site	Nonmetro	Unit
I	AZ DC FL GA LA MA MD MI NY OH PA RI TN TX WA	0.19 (0.06)	0.75 (0.07)	0.06 (0.04)	0.04 (0.04)
II	AR DE HI IA IL IN KY KS NE NM MN MO OK WI WV	0.02 (0.02)	0.94 (0.04)	0.05 (0.04)	0.16 (0.02)
III	CO MT WY	0.06 (0.04)	0.69 (0.21)	0.25 (0.17)	0.50 (0.26)
IV	NC SC VA	0.38 (0.06)	0.37 (0.06)	0.25 (0.04)	0.01 (0.01)
V	AL CA CT NJ NV	0.39 (0.08)	0.54 (0.04)	0.07 (0.05)	0.02 (0.01)
VI	NH ND OR SD UT	0.15 (0.06)	0.63 (0.09)	0.22 (0.03)	0.23 (0.20)
VII	AK ID ME MS VT	0.11 (0.07)	0.52 (0.12)	0.44 (0.10)	0.00 (0.00)
US		0.22	0.72	0.06	0.08

*: The first entries in each cell are percentages of total deposit. Entries in parentheses are standard deviations.

Table 5.2 Cluster Structure Based on Number of Operating Units*

Cluster	State	Out-Flow	On-Site	Nonmetro	Unit
I	AZ DC FL GA LA MA MD MI NY OH PA RI TN TX WA	0.22 (0.06)	0.69 (0.07)	0.09 (0.05)	0.03 (0.04)
II	AR DE HI IA IL IN KY KS NE NM MN MO OK WI WV	0.03 (0.02)	0.88 (0.08)	0.10 (0.07)	0.12 (0.02)
III	CO MT WY	0.03 (0.02)	0.77 (0.19)	0.20 (0.18)	0.54 (0.21)
IV	NC SC VA	0.40 (0.06)	0.30 (0.01)	0.30 (0.06)	0.01 (0.01)
V	AL CA CT NJ NV	0.44 (0.10)	0.47 (0.04)	0.09 (0.07)	0.02 (0.01)
VI	NH ND OR SD UT	0.15 (0.07)	0.58 (0.09)	0.28 (0.05)	0.06 (0.05)
VII	AK ID ME MS VT	0.04 (0.06)	0.36 (0.09)	0.59 (0.10)	0.00 (0.00)
US		0.27	0.63	0.10	0.05

*: Entries in each cell are percentage of total operating units. Entries in parentheses are standard deviations.

Table 5.3 Structural Quotients

Cluster	State	Out-Flow	On-Site	Nonmetro	Unit
I	AZ DC FL GA LA MA MD MI NY	0.86*	1.04	1.11	0.47
	OH PA RI TN TX WA	0.81	1.10	0.90	0.68
II	AR DE HI IA IL IN KY KS NE NM	0.09	1.30	0.84	1.91
	MN MO OK WI WV	0.12	1.40	0.92	2.46
III	CO MT WY	0.26	0.96	4.37	6.11
		0.13	1.22	1.89	10.48
IV	NC SC VA	1.73	0.51	4.32	0.17
		1.51	0.47	2.86	0.24
V	AL CA CT NJ NV	1.76	0.75	1.18	0.23
		1.65	0.75	0.87	0.44
VI	NH ND OR SD UT	0.67	0.88	3.83	2.79
		0.55	0.92	2.67	0.95
VII	AK ID ME MS VT	0.50	0.72	7.69	0.09
		0.17	0.58	5.68	0.07

*: The first entries in each cell are structural quotients based on amount of deposits. The second are based on number of operating units.

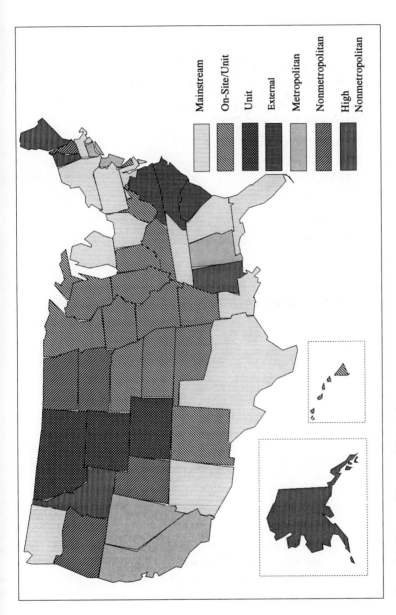

Figure 5.1 Clusters of Structural Orientations

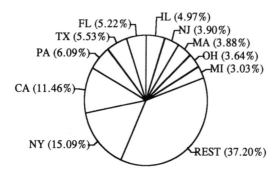

Percent of state metropolitan total deposits
in national metropolitan total deposits

Figure 5.2 Top Ten States in Total Metropolitan Deposits

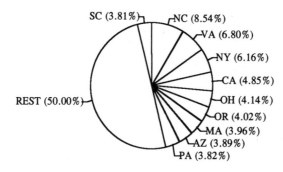

Percent of state nonmetropolitan
deposits in national nonmetropolitan
deposits

Figure 5.3 Top Ten States in Nonmetropolitan Banking Ownership

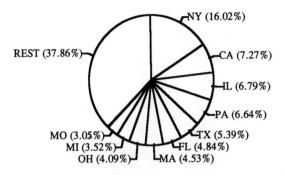

Percent of state metropolitan on-site deposits in national metropolitanon-site deposits

Figure 5.4 Top Ten States in Metropolitan On-site Banking Ownership

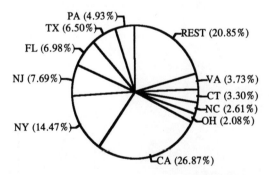

Percent of state metropolitan out-flow deposits in national metropolitan out-flow deposits

Figure 5.5 Top Ten States in Metropolitan Out-flow Banking Ownership

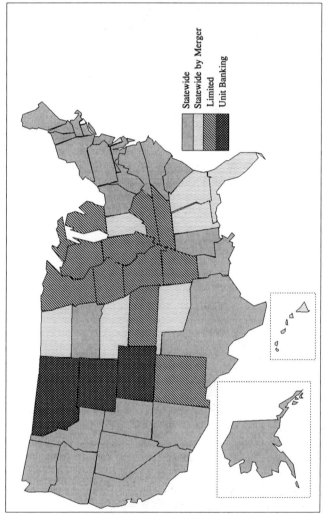

Figure 5.6 State Branch Banking Law as of 1991

is therefore a result of an extensive economy and branch legislative status.

Cluster II: On-site/Unit Banking Structural Orientation. With a few exceptions, most systems in this cluster are in the Midwest and Plain states where, traditionally, the agricultural economy and resultant locally scattered communities have contributed to the strong attachment to the unit banking system. Although various legislative changes have taken place, limitations on branching still exist. Using U.S. metropolitan averages as means, the null hypothesis is rejected at the 0.995 level for on-site, and at the 0.9 level for unit banking. The high structural quotients in these two categories illustrate their distinct structural feature. All states in this cluster, except Colorado, are among the top ten in terms of on-site ownership measured by percentage of deposits (Figure 5.7). An important aspect of such orientation is extremely low levels of out-flow. The average structural quotient in this category is only 0.11.

Cluster III: Unit Banking Orientation. All three states in this cluster have a unit banking legislative status (Figure 5.6). Therefore, the highest structural quotient in unit ownership and a low structural quotient in out-flow category result. However, large standard deviations indicate that there are wide variations among these three states. In addition, the higher than average percentage in nonmetropolitan ownership indicates variations in branch limitations. Nonetheless, the three states in this cluster rank the first (Colorado), fourth (Montana) and sixth (Wyoming) in unit banking percentage among all states with more than one metropolitan area (Figure 5.8). Another common characteristic among the three is the lower than average percentage in out-flow, an indication of a poorly connected metropolitan system through branch banking function.

Cluster IV: External Orientation. In this cluster, all percentages vary significantly from U.S. metropolitan averages (the null hypothesis is rejected at the 0.95 level for all categories). Structural quotients are significantly larger than one in terms of out-flow and nonmetropolitan ownerships. This is the only cluster in which the percentage in out-flow is larger than that in on-site. States in this cluster have similar branching legislative status. More distinctively, they are also geographically close to each other. All states in this group are among the top ten in out-flow and nonmetropolitan ownership measured by percentages of total deposits (Figure 5.9 and Figure 5.10). This structural orientation indicates strong ties between metropolitan areas

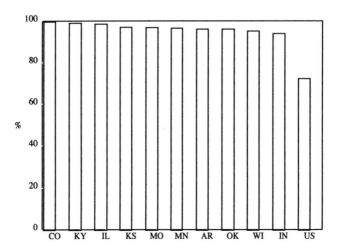

Figure 5.7 Top Ten States in On-site Ownership: Percent of
On-site Deposits in Total Deposits

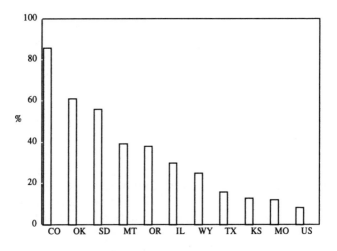

Figure 5.8 Top Ten States in Unit Bank Ownership: Percent
of Unit Bank Deposits in Total Deposits

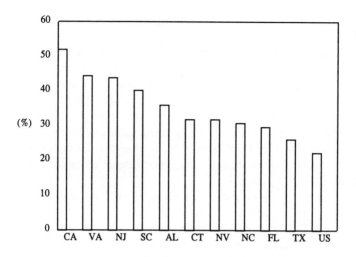

Figure 5.9 Top Ten States in Out-flow Ownership: Percent
of Out-flow Deposits in Total Deposits

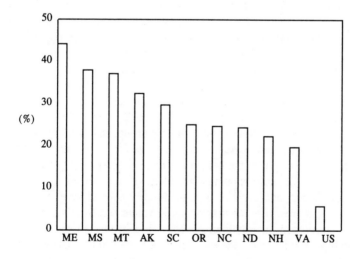

Figure 5.10 Top Ten States in Nonmetropolitan Ownership:
Percent of Nonmetropolitan Deposits in Total
Deposits

and between metropolitan areas and nonmetropolitan areas. High out-flow and low unit banking quotients indicate an extensive branch network.

Cluster V: Metropolitan Orientation. All states in this cluster are within the top ten out-flow ownership systems measured by the percentage of deposits (Figure 5.9). Connection across metropolitan areas is the most important characteristic that distinguishes this cluster from others. Compared with cluster IV, the connection to nonmetropolitan areas is much weaker (as a matter of fact, the null hypothesis cannot even be rejected at the 0.75 level). This orientation features a well connected metropolitan system through a branch banking network.

Cluster VI: Nonmetropolitan Orientation. The most distinct feature of this cluster is a larger than average nonmetropolitan connection, with an on-site percentage close to the U.S. metropolitan average (the difference is insignificant at the 0.95 level). Three out of five states in this cluster are among the top ten states in terms of nonmetropolitan ownership measured by the percentage of total deposits (Figure 5.10). Although geographically diverse, all states in the cluster have similar branch legislative status and the sizes of their economies are comparable. The difference in percentages when comparing deposit amount and number of offices in this cluster is mainly due to the location of CitiBank in South Dakota. Citibank has only one operational site but accounts for 55.5% of deposits in South Dakota.

Cluster VII: High Nonmetropolitan Orientation. Compared with Cluster VI, this cluster exhibits a much higher nonmetropolitan percentage (actually the highest among all clusters), with an on-site percentage significantly different from the U.S. metropolitan average at the 0.95 level. All state systems in this group, that have more than one metropolitan area, are among the top ten in nonmetropolitan ownership measured by the percentage of total deposits (Figure 5.10). In addition, the unit banking percentage is the lowest among all clusters. Three out of five systems in this cluster have only one metropolitan area. The other two states, Maine and Mississippi, have poorly developed metropolitan systems. In addition, all states have a legislative status that allows statewide branching. Under such circumstances, a strong tie between metropolitan banks and nonmetropolitan areas is a natural result. The major features of the seven clusters of structural orientation discussed above are briefly summarized in Table 5.4.

Table 5.4 Summary of Clusters of Structural Orientations

Cluster	State	Orientation	Representations in Structural Categories			
			Out-Flow	On-Site	Nonmetro	Unit
I	AZ DC FL GA LA MA MD MI NY OH PA RI TN TX WA	Mainstream	Ave	Ave	Ave	Low
II	AR DE HI IA IL IN KS KY MN MO NE NM OK WI WV	On-Site/Unit	LOW*	HIGH	Ave	High
III	CO MT WY	Unit	Low	Ave	High	HIGH
IV	NC SC VA	External	High	LOW	High	Low
V	AL CA CT NJ NV	Metro	HIGH	Ave	Ave	Low
VI	NH ND OR SD UT	Nonmetro	Low	Ave	High	-*
VII	AK ID ME MS VT	High Nonmetro	Low	Low	HIGH	LOW

* : "-" Indicates the inconsistent results based on deposit amount and number of offices.
** : "Capitalized" indicates the highest or lowest across clusters.

Hierarchical Structure of Metropolitan Banking Systems Under Branch Banking Network

Out-flows of branch banking corporate ownership across metropolitan areas constitute the ties between places. The magnitude of these ties and the position of each metropolitan area involved form a hierarchy of places in the banking field. A generally weak intermetropolitan branch connection results in fragmentation. Such fragmentation will necessarily affect the hierarchical structure of places. At the national level, since 50 state branch banking systems have developed in isolation, a national hierarchy of the branch banking network does not exist. As a result, the study of the hierarchical structure of the branch bank network lies mainly at the state level. The study of structure contains two steps: disclosure of the hierarchical structure, and a typology analysis of the hierarchical structure. These analyses provide a basic foundation for understanding the relationship between spatial and hierarchical structures in metropolitan banking networks.

Hierarchical Structure of the Branch Banking Network. Dominant-flow principles are used to discover the state metropolitan banking hierarchy under the branch banking system. Figures 5.11 to 5.14 provide two examples. Figure 5.11 shows the hierarchical structure for California. The arrows in the diagram show the direction of subordination. The number associated with the arrows shows the magnitude of the ties between places, and the numbers in the place boxes show the total deposits related to a particular place's order, as explained in the first section of this chapter. The unit used is millions of dollars. For example, San Francisco owns 1,311 million dollars of deposits in Oakland, while Oakland owns 63 million dollars of deposits in San Francisco. San Francisco is a higher order place than Oakland because it has more total deposits related to it (120,000 million dollars) than Oakland (17,280 million dollars). Figure 5.12 illustrates this hierarchy on a map to reveal the relationship between hierarchy and geography in the banking field. Figures 5.13 and 5.14 display the same information for Colorado. Mapping the hierarchical structures for 50 states results in Figure 5.15, which clearly demonstrates the geographic fragmentation of banking corporate ownership networks under branch ownership. Within a state, the metropolitan system is more or less

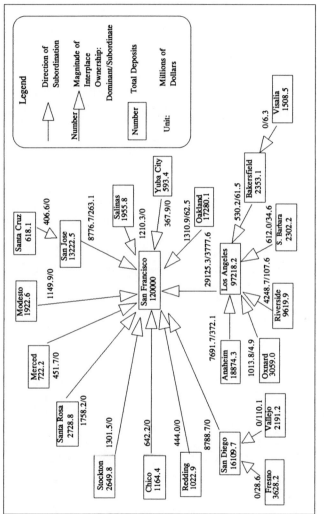

Figure 5.11 Branch Banking Hierarchical Network: California

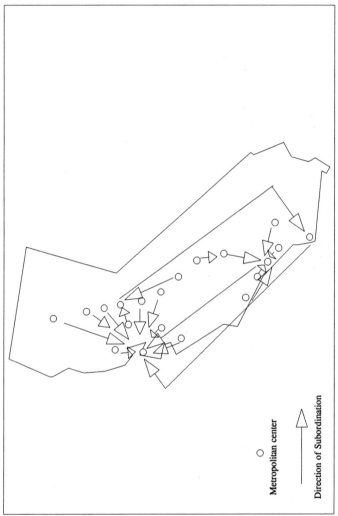

Metropolitan center

Direction of Subordination

Figure 5.12 The Branch Banking Network: California

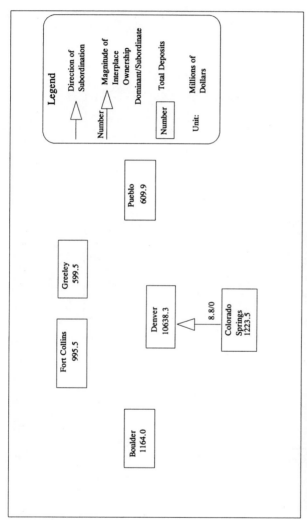

Figure 5.13 Branch Banking Hierarchical Network: Colorado

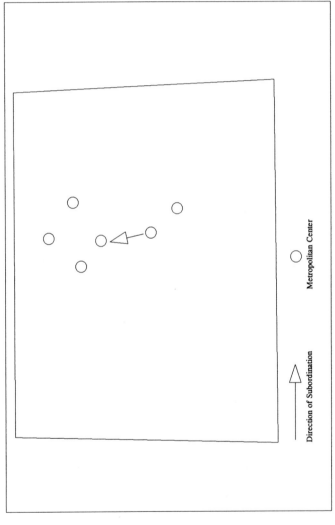

Figure 5.14 The Branch Banking Network: Colorado

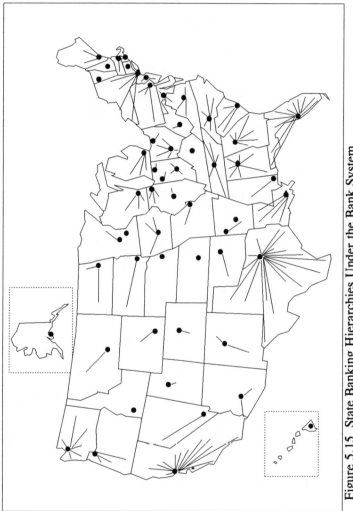

Figure 5.15 State Banking Hierarchies Under the Bank System

connected through branch ownership. Between states, there exists legal barriers that keep the 50 states separate in terms of branch ownership.

Typology of the State Banking Hierarchical Structure. As shown in Figures 5.11 and 5.13, great differences exist between state hierarchical structures. Such differences can be systematically detected using a typology approach developed in Appendix B. Three major types and seven sub-types are identified. The three major types are single, connected, and disconnected. The single type means there is only one center in a network. A disconnected system indicates there is more than one component in a system. A connected system means the hierarchical network is a digraph minimally connected. The seven sub-types are single, centralized, centralized/hierarchical, hierarchical, simple connected, null, and disjointed. The second to fifth types are minimally connected. The sixth and seventh are disconnected. A simple description of the seven sub-types is given in Figure 5.16. Table 5.5 lists state systems that fall in the different types.

In a centralized system, the center at the top of hierarchy has maximum flows with all metropolitan areas in the system. Thus, the dominance of the top center is realized through its direct linkages with all centers in the system. In contrast, in a well-developed hierarchical structure, metropolitan areas have the maximum flow with higher order centers in proximity, forming extensive sub-hub systems. The top center realizes its dominance through the maximum flows with these sub-centers and other metropolitan areas. This constitutes co-existence of multiple important centers in a banking system. In a centralized hierarchical structure, a dominant top-order center and less extensive sub-systems co-exist.

The disjointed group can be further analyzed by calculating the hierarchical and centrality indices for components in networks, resulting in disjointed simple connected, disjointed centralized, etc. In case that two components have indices that result in a conflicting classification (e.g. one component is centralized and the other hierarchical), the disjointed mixed type is assigned. The sub-groups within the disjointed type are listed in Table 5.6.

Table 5.5 Types of Hierarchical Structure

Type of Hierarchical Structure		State System	Criteria
Major	Sub-type		
Single	Single	AK DE HI ID VT	$V=1$
Connected	Simple Connected	MT NV RI SD UT WY	$V=2$, $H_c=1$
	Centralized	AZ NH ME NM ND OR WA	$H_c=1$, $c_m=1$ or $H_c<1.5$ & $c_m<2$
	Centralized/ Hierarchical	AL GA LA MA MI SC TN	$H_c>1.5$ & $c_m<2$ or $H_c<1.5$ & $c_m>2$
	Hierarchical	CA CT FL MD NC NJ NY	$H_c>1.5$ & $c_m>2$
Disconnected	Null	KS KY NE	$H_c=0$, $c_m=0$, $P=1$
	Disjointed	AR CO IA IL IN MN OH MO OK PA TX WI WV MS	$P<v$

SINGLE

A single center with no connections

NULL

Multiple centers with no connections

SIMPLE CONNECTED

Two centers with a single connection

DISJOINTED

The network contains more than one component

CENTRALIZED

One center serves as a hub into which connections
converge

HIERARCHICAL

Multiple centers in a hierarchical system

CENTRALIZED HIERARCHICAL

Hierarchical complex. Several hierachies combined
in a single system

Figure 5.16 Typology of Hierarchical Networks

Table 5.6 Sub-groups in Disjointed Hierarchical Sub-type

Sub-group	State
Disjointed Simple	AR CO MN MO MS WV
Disjointed Mixed	IL IN PA WI
Disjointed Central	IA
Disjointed Central/Hierarchical	OH TX
Disjointed Hierarchical	OK

Relationships Between Spatial and Hierarchical Structures

Having independently obtained the spatial and hierarchical structures for state metropolitan banking networks, the relationship between these two structures can be analyzed by examining the correspondence between particular structural orientations and hierarchical types. This can be done by tabulating state metropolitan banking systems in a two-way table. While Table 5.7 lists seven clusters and the disjointed type, Table 5.8 lists the seven clusters and the connected type. The seven clusters are ordered so that the out-flow level decreases across clusters. Therefore, in Tables 5.7 and 5.8, moving from the top to the bottom rows, the banking connections between metropolitan areas become weaker in terms of out-flow percentage in the total metropolitan-owned deposits. Moving from the left to right columns, the structures become more hierarchical. Virginia is not listed because Washington D.C. is included in the hierarchical network of Virginia, hence this blurs the state metropolitan hierarchical picture.

Several characteristics of metropolitan banking networks stand out. First, all systems that have either external or metropolitan orientations are either hierarchical or centralized hierarchical in

Table 5.7 Clusters of Structural Orientations and Disconnected Hierarchical Structure

Cluster	Hierarchical Type					
	1	2	3	4	5	6
V						
IV						
I			PA		TX OH	
VI						
VII						
II	KS KY NE	WV MN MO AR MS	IL IN WI	IA		OK
III		CO				

1. Null
2. Disjointed Simple Connected
3. Disjointed Mixed
4. Disjointed Central
5. Disjointed Central/Hierarchical
6. Disjointed Hierarchical

Table 5.8 Clusters of Structural Orientations and Connected Hierarchical Structure

Cluster	Hierarchical Type			
	7	8	9	10
V	NV		AL	CA CT NJ
IV			SC	NC
I	RI	AZ WA	GA LA MA MI TN	FL NY MD
VI	SD UT	NH ND OR		
VII		ME		
II		NM		
III	MT WY			

7. Simple Connected
8. Centralized
9. Central/Hierarchical
10. Hierarchical

terms of typology. The majority of systems in the mainstream orientation are hierarchical, centralized hierarchical, or are their disjointed counterparts. Second, with Oklahoma as an exception, none of the systems in on-site/unit, nonmetropolitan, and unit orientations have developed hierarchical, centralized hierarchical, or their disjointed counterparts in terms of typologies. The vast majority of systems with these orientations are either disjointed, simple connected or disjointed mixed. At the extreme are the three null structures. Generally speaking, the Midwest states, Prairie states, and northeast Mountain states have poorly developed branch banking networks while the East and West coastal states, especially those large states, have developed well connected state branch network systems.

The above patterns indicate that state branch banking legislation and sizes of state metropolitan systems significantly contribute to the spatial and hierarchical structures of place banking networks. Metropolitan areas generally have a high concentration of economic activities. These are accompanied by active monetary flows within and between metropolitan areas. Thus, the size of a state metropolitan system provides a structural foundation for possible banking connections between places. A large state metropolitan system is likely to generate a high volume of monetary flows between metropolitan areas. These across metropolitan monetary flows are mediated by various financial institutions. For a state that allows statewide branching, monetary flows between metropolitan areas can be mediated by banking facilities that belong to the same banks. The aggregate banking place network based on branch banking ownership is likely to be spatially connected and hierarchically developed. When branch banking legislation is restrictive, the monetary flows between metropolitan areas are likely to be mediated by banking facilities that belong to different banks. Thus, the aggregate place banking network based on branch banking ownership is likely to be poorly connected.

SPATIAL AND HIERARCHICAL STRUCTURES OF CORPORATE BANKING UNDER THE BANK HOLDING SYSTEM

Spatial corporate banking networks under bank holding companies (BHCs) largely represent a higher level of banking ownership between places compared with the branch banking relationship. Although generally not considered as an operating unit, bank holding companies can still affect operations of member banks in various ways as discussed previously. The banking network under bank holding is an important component in intermetropolitan banking linkages, and is therefore extremely important in understanding spatial structures of interstate banking. This section examines to what extent the regulatory wall to interstate banking has been brought down under the bank holding system. Specifically, changes in the connectivity of spatial banking networks brought about by the bank holding relationship and the remaining problems with such networks will be investigated.

As of early 1991, 612 bank holding companies were headquartered in metropolitan areas. These companies controlled 4,393 metropolitan banks, 33,476 banking offices, and 1,356,839.8 million dollars in deposits. In other words, 79.8% of metropolitan banks, 73.7% of banking offices, and 63.6% of deposits were owned by bank holding companies headquartered in the metropolitan system. Among all bank holding ownerships, 594,291.5 million dollars in deposits (43.8%), or 14,763 banking offices (44.1%), are located in the same metropolitan areas where the bank holding companies are headquartered; 670,273.9 million dollars in deposits (49.4%), or 15,299 banking offices (45.7%), are under intermetropolitan ownership. The rest, 92265.1 million dollars in deposits (6.8%), or 3,415 banking offices (10.2%), have metropolitan-rural connections. In other words, over half the bank holding connections occur between places. This compares with 22.2% of deposits and 26.6% of offices in branch ownership that have intermetropolitan connections. This difference in intermetropolitan connection will necessarily bring significant changes to the general spatial and hierarchical structures of the banking corporate landscape.

Differences in Intrastate Connectivity

The first significant difference concerns the connectivity of the intrastate metropolitan banking system under bank holding companies (BHCs). Of 1110 entries in the BHC bank ownership matrix, 475 are intrastate entries. More than one third, i.e., 164, of the intrastate entries occur between those pairs of metropolitan areas that have not been connected under the branch system. The other 311 entries repeat branch entries. This increases the total intrastate entries to 935, resulting in a intrastate density of 0.2468, a 21.3% increase from 0.2034. Of the 164 new entries, 42.7%, or 70, occur in those states with On-site/Unit and Unit structural orientations. Table 5.9 illustrates that in most of these states, the total intrastate entries under bank holding is greater than under branch banking. The single most important source of these higher entries is new connections between places formed under the bank holding relationship. In most of the states, new entries under BHC account for the greatest share in total intrastate degree, and are greater than the total entries under the branch system. For the rest of the states, total intrastate entries under BHC are smaller than those under the branch system. Because of increases in intermetropolitan connections within the state metropolitan system, the intrastate intermetropolitan deposits ownership in total state deposits are likely to increase. Of 19 states that experience an increase in out-flow ownership within their state metropolitan systems, 13 are states with On-site/Unit or Unit structural orientations and they have the highest out-flow increase in terms of percentages (Table 5.10).

New entries in the intrastate across metropolitan banking ownership matrix significantly changed the hierarchical structures for those states in which these new entries occurred. Of the 17 states which have disconnected hierarchical structures in Table 5.6, 10 changed to a connected structure within the bank holding system (Table 5.11). Figure 5.17 shows the hierarchical structure under the BHC system for Colorado. Compared with Figure 5.13, the increase in connectivity is significant.

Table 5.9 Comparison of Total Intrastate Entries[*]

Cluster	State	Entry B	Entry BHC	New Entry
I	AZ	2	2	0
	FL	82	24	4
	GA	11	11	4
	LA	15	6	0
	MA	23	13	0
	MD	6	2	0
	MI	23	36	18
	NY	53	32	6
	OH	35	32	12
	PA	45	39	19
	RI	2	2	0
	TN	10	11	0
	TX	64	35	16
	WA	16	12	1
II	AR	2	2	2
	IA	3	5	4
	IL	7	13	9
	IN	11	12	10
	KS	0	3	3
	KY	0	2	2
	MN	2	4	3
	MO	1	10	10
	NE	0	1	1
	NM	2	2	0
	OK	3	1	0
	WI	7	16	13
	WV	3	4	3

Table 5.9 Comparison of Total Intrastate Entries (Cont'd)

Cluster	State	Entry B	Entry BHC	New Entry
III	CO	2	11	9
	MT	1	0	0
	WY	1	0	0
IV	NC	26	20	0
	SC	12	4	1
	VA	12	12	5
V	AL	19	18	6
	CA	150	29	3
	CT	50	13	0
	NJ	39	20	5
	NV	2	1	0
VI	ND	2	0	0
	NH	4	2	0
	OR	6	3	0
	SD	1	0	0
	UT	2	1	0
VII	ME	2	0	0
	MS	2	2	0

*: This table contains only states with more than one metropolitan area
Entry B: Total intrastate entries under the branch system
Entry BHC: Total intrastate entries under the bank holding system
New Entry: Entries under the bank holding system that do not exist under the branch system

Table 5.10 Changes in Out-flow for States that Experience an Increase

State	BRANCH	BHC	Change (%)
KS*	0.0	10.9	**
NE*	0.0	8.7	**
KY*	0.0	2.7	**
MO*	0.08	18.3	22787.5
CO*	0.08	15.8	19700.0
MN*	0.05	6.8	13420.0
AR*	0.64	7.3	1043.8
WI*	3.2	15.5	373.5
IL*	1.3	5.3	309.2
IN*	2.4	7.4	209.7
NM*	2.3	6.1	161.6
OH	12.7	32.6	156.5
WV*	4.6	10.7	133.6
MI	11.5	24.8	115.3
MA	10.2	12.8	25.4
OK*	1.9	2.4	25.4
AL	35.9	41.2	14.7
NH	20.0	22.6	12.7
PA	18.0	19.2	7.0

BRANCH: Share of intrastate outflows in total state deposits under branch system
BHC: Share of intrastate outflows in total state deposits under BHC system
*: States in On-Site/Unit and Unit structural orientations
**: Change from zero to current level

Table 5.11   Changes in States with Disconnected
Hierarchical Structure under the BHC

State	Branch System	BHC System
AR	Disjointed Simple Connected	Disjointed Centralized
CO	Disjointed Simple Connected	Hierarchical
IA	Disjointed Centralized	Disjointed Central/Hierarchical
IL	Disjointed Mixed	Disjointed Central/Hierarchical
IN	Disjointed Mixed	Disjointed Central/Hierarchical
KS	Null	Centralized
KY	Null	Centralized
MM	Disjointed Simple Connected	Central/Hierarchical
MO	Disjointed Simple Connected	Central/Hierarchical
MS	Disjointed Simple Connected	Hierarchical
NE	Null	Simple Connected
OH	Disjointed Central/Hierarchical	Hierarchical
OK	Disjointed Hierarchical	No Improvement
PA	Disjointed Mixed	Disjointed Central/Hierarchical
TX	Disjointed Central/Hierarchical	No Improvement
WI	Disjointed Mixed	Central/Hierarchical
WV	Disjointed Simple Connected	Central/Hierarchical

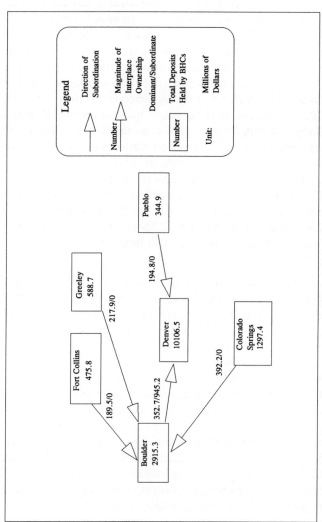

Figure 5.17 Bank Holding Company Hierarchical Network: Colorado

Characteristics of Interstate Bank Holding

The most significant change to the banking landscape brought about by the bank holding system is interstate bank holding. Since the total matrix degree increases from 772 to 1,110, the density of the metropolitan system increases to 0.0099. This density is 1.4 times that of the branch network matrix. Of 1,110 intermetropolitan connections, 653, or 58.8% are across state intermetropolitan connections. With the maximum possible number of cross-state intermetropolitan connections at 108,094, this results in a cross-state intermetropolitan density of 0.006. Compared with the zero cross state entry in the branch matrix, this is a significant change. These 653 entries brought 397.2 billion dollars in deposits and 8,349 banking offices under cross state intermetropolitan ownership. These account for 59.3% of total deposits or 54.5% of the total number of offices under intermetropolitan ownership, 29.3% of total deposits and 24.9% of total banking offices under bank holding ownership, and 17.6% of total deposits and 18.4% of total banking offices in the entire U.S metropolitan system.

Spatial and hierarchical patterns of interstate banking. The research findings pertaining to interstate banking patterns can be summarized in three areas. First, there is a distinct geographic distribution of interstate acquiring and target states. To examine each state's role in interstate intermetropolitan banking activity, six pairs of structural indices are defined in Table 5.12. Ward's minimum distance cluster analysis is applied to these 12 variables. Groupings from the clustering operations on variables and the first four principal components of the variables are slightly different. The grouping from the clustering operation on variables is adopted because some groupings from the alternative approach do not entirely conform to the reality. For example, according to principle component clustering, California is in the same cluster with Rhode Island and Oregon. California has enormous bank holding within and outside the state metropolitan system, compared with the limited intrastate metropolitan systems of Rhode Island and Oregon. Such a grouping is therefore less than satisfactory. Another anomalous example is that as a major dominant center in out-of-state bank holding in New England, the state of Massachusetts is inappropriately grouped,

Table 5.12 Structural Variables Used in the Cluster Analysis*

BHC	Total bank holding activity to total banking measured by both number of offices and amount of deposits
OWN	Portion of deposits and offices owned by bank holding companies located in the same metropolitan area
OI	Portion of deposits and offices owned by bank holding companies located in different metropolitan areas but in the same state
OO	Portion of deposits and offices held by bank holding companies owned in one state but located in metropolitan areas of other states
IO	Portion of deposits and offices located in one state but owned by bank holding companies in other states and headquartered in metropolitan areas
NON	Portion of deposits and offices in nonmetropolitan areas owned by bank holding companies headquartered in metropolitan areas

*: Since each variable can be constructed with the amount of deposits and the number of banking offices, there are totally 12 structural variables.

using principle component clustering, in the same cluster with New Hampshire, one of the major acquisition targets for Massachusetts.

Ten clusters are obtained. Calculating average values of the above deposit ratios for each cluster and using average values for all states as references, structural quotients for each cluster are obtained for each ratio (Table 5.13). In terms of interstate banking, three major groups can be identified. States in clusters I to IV have the largest shares of banking deposits held by out-of-state bank holding companies, and therefore are important interstate banking targets. States in clusters VI to IX, plus states in cluster IV hold the largest share of out-of-state deposits, and thus are important acquirers of out-of-state banking facilities. States in clusters V and X are generally not active interstate banking participants. Wide variations exist within each group. For example, Cluster IV occurs in both target and acquirer groups, and Cluster X shows slight activity in interstate expansion. The characteristics with respect to interstate banking for each cluster are highlighted in Table 5.14. The largest concentration of interstate acquiring states lies in the North and Southeast, in a region extending from Massachusetts, south to Virginia and North Carolina, and west across the upper Great Lakes to Minnesota. In addition, three less coherent concentrations of interstate acquiring states are found in Alabama, Missouri, and California. Interstate target states encompass large areas of the United States, extending from Washington in the Northwest, and forming a wide band across the mid-section of the country. In addition, target states are seen in the Midwest from Iowa to Indiana, in the upper south from West Virginia to Tennessee, and in the extreme southeast of the country. Isolated target states can also be observed among the northeastern coastal states.

In terms of absolute values, states with large populations tend to dominate in every category. Table 5.15 lists the top ten states in each of the five categories. The importance of states can be partly seen from the number of appearances of states in different categories. New York and California occur in all five categories. North Carolina, Massachusetts, Ohio, and Pennsylvania appear in four out of five categories. Connecticut and Minnesota are in three categories. Virginia, Georgia, Florida, Michigan, and New Jersey, appear in two categories. In interstate banking, New York, California, and Georgia hold   large   deposits   in   other   states   but   also   have   a   large amount of deposits held by other states. North Carolina, Virginia,

Table 5.13 Structural Quotients in Bank Holding

Cluster	State	BHC	OWN	OI	OO	IO	NON
I	AK DE ME ND SC SD WV WA	0.49	0.12	0.05	0.10	2.51	0.08
II	AZ FL KY NV TN TX	0.92	0.58	0.91	0.11	1.79	0.37
III	CO HI IA IL IN MT NE NM OK	0.61	1.29	1.09	0.11	1.17	0.24
IV	CT DC GA OR	1.29	0.80	0.31	1.31	1.36	0.53
V	AR KS NH UT VT WY	0.73	2.03	1.45	0.47	0.17	1.01
VI	LA NY MI MO PA WI	1.03	1.70	1.06	1.10	0.49	0.25
VII	MA MD MN	1.50	1.38	1.40	2.33	0.08	1.13
VIII	AL NJ OH	0.86	0.88	2.85	1.49	0.43	0.54
IX	NC VA CA RI	2.78	0.43	0.84	4.79	0.12	1.76
X	ID MS	1.00	0.87	0.61	1.05	0.61	7.92

Variables from columns 3 to 8 are defined in Table 5.12.

Table 5.14 Characteristics of States in Interstate Banking

Cluster	State	Description
I	AK DE ME ND SC SD WV WA	Interstate banking targets
II	AZ FL KY NV TN TX	Interstate banking targets; Stronger in intrastate expansion than Cluster I
III	CO HI IA IL IN MT NE NM OK	Interstate banking targets; Strong on-site and stronger intrastate expansions
IV	CT DC GA OR	Interstate banking targets; Interstate banking acquirers
V	AR KS NH UT VT WY	Inactive in interstate banking; Strong on-site and intrastate expansions
VI	LA MI NY MO PA WI	Interstate banking acquirers; Strong on-site and slightly strong intrastate expansion
VII	MA MD MN	Interstate banking acquirers; Strong on-site and intrastate expansions
VIII	AL NJ OH	Interstate banking acquirers; Strong intrastate expansion
IX	NC VA CA RI	Interstate banking acquirers
X	ID MS	Strong expansion in Nonmetropolitan areas; Slightly strong interstate acquirers

Massachusetts, Ohio, New Jersey, and Minnesota are large holders of deposits in other states. Texas, Florida, Washington D.C., Arizona, Pennsylvania, Delaware, and Connecticut have the largest accounts held by other states.

Table 5.15 Top Ten States In Bank Holding Activities

Category	State
Interstate banking acquirers	CA NC NY VA MA OH GA NJ MN CT
Interstate banking targets	TX CA FL DC GA AZ PA DE NY CT
On-site holding	NY IL CA PA MI MA OH MN MD NC
Nonmetropolitan expansion	NC VA MA CA NY MN OH PA UT CT
Intrastate expansion	NY CA OH PA NJ FL MI NC MA AL

Second, interstate banking command/control fields demonstrate spatially skewed and regionally focused characteristics. If metropolitan areas within a state are consolidated into a single unit, a 51-by-51 interstate banking matrix can be constructed where entries on the matrix are interstate bank holdings (deposits). Bank holding between any pair of states can be used to calculate Wheeler's C-value. The C-value expresses the magnitude of command/control of a particular location. In the current context, this amounts to seeking net banking ownership out-flow. This gives the magnitude of one place's command/control power over one another.[4] Figure 5.18 displays the command/control fields for the 10 largest command and control states in terms of the number of states controlled.

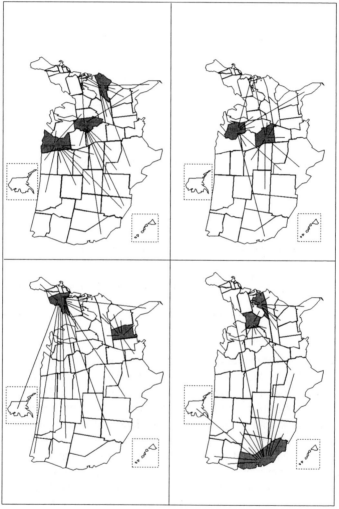

Figure 5.18   Interstate Banking Command/Control Fields of the Top 10 States

The spatially skewed pattern is most typical of New York's, and to a lesser extent, Illinois's, interstate banking command/control fields. New York's command/control field is heavily concentrated in western states, but conspicuously absent from the western section of the Midwest, all New England states except Maine, and all southern states except Florida. In a similar fashion, Illinois's banking field mainly extends westward, leaving a scant presence in the East and the South. The regionally focused pattern is characteristic of most other interstate banking command/control fields such as California, Minnesota, North Carolina, Ohio, and Alabama. Distant interstate banking entries are generally confined to western states.

Spatially skewed and regionally focused patterns can be largely attributed to the regional banking that characterized interstate banking until the early 1990s (Miller 1990a). Regional compacts prevented New York banks from interstate acquisitions in the Midwest, New England, and Southeast. A similar mechanism prevented Chicago banks from entering the Southeast and New England. Regional banking caused regional bank mergers and acquisitions. The most important example is the merger of the North Carolina NCNB bank with the Georgia and Virginia based C&S/Sovran bank, forming the nation's third largest bank holding company, the NationsBank. Other examples include BankAmerica's merger with the Security Pacific Bank, Chemical Bank's merger with Manufactures Hanover Bank, and the Keycorp's merger with Security Trust. All these gigantic bank mergers occurred within regions or between nearby states. Meanwhile, many western states adopted national banking laws allowing distant banking entries. The result is banking consolidation on a regional basis, and the forced westward expansion of New York banks.

Third, when the principles of dominant flow are applied to the 335-by-335 metropolitan matrix of banking ownership under bank holding companies, fifteen interstate banking hierarchical systems are identified. Each system is centered on a metropolitan area and is composed of a certain number of metropolitan areas extending to a number of states. Since these systems are identified on the basis of the maximum flow among them, the connection within each system is greater than between systems. These systems are independent of each other in that the top or central metropolitan area of one system is not subordinate to any other metropolitan area according to the principles of dominant flow. In other words, it is a true independent center.

Figure 5.19 provides a simplified illustration of these fifteen system, which contains the fifteen top centers and states involved in each of the systems.

In addition to these 15 independent interstate banking hierarchical systems, three West Virginian metropolitan areas, Charleston, Huntington, and Wheeling, form an independent intrastate hierarchical system with Charleston at the top of the hierarchy. Wichita, Kansas is not hierarchically associated with any system. Finally, 7 metropolitan areas stand alone, truly independent of any other systems. Of the 7 centers, Dubuque and Iowa City, Iowa, Fort Smith, Arkansas, Lawton, Oklahoma, and Texarkana, Texas have only on-site banking holding expansion. Enid, Oklahoma, and Erie, Pennsylvania, do not have any kind of banking holding activities.

The fifteen interstate banking hierarchical systems indicate the existence of sub-systems in regional banking compacts. Although a regional banking compact is defined as an interstate banking unit in most interstate banking literature (Rose 1989; Miller 1990a), the hierarchies of centers indicate that a regional banking compact may break down into sub-systems. Examples of such subsystems are the Columbus, Detroit, Chicago, and Minneapolis systems in the Midwest compact, and the Norfolk, Charlotte, and Birmingham systems in the Southeast compact. This may be largely due to the co-existence of major banking centers within a banking compact. On the other hand, in the West and New England, only one center has overwhelming dominance. As a result, centers in the entire region fall into a unified hierarchical system.

Identification of the interstate banking hierarchical systems helps demonstrate dominance of regional banking centers over money centers in interstate banking. The above discussion has shown that California, Minnesota, New York, and Illinois all have extensive banking fields in the west. However, the New York and Chicago hierarchical systems have very few western metropolitan areas in their systems, in contrast to a strong presence of western states in the San Francisco and Minneapolis systems. This indicates that hierarchically western metropolitan areas are more closely tied to San Francisco and Minneapolis. The advantages of regional banks over money center banks in interstate banking have directly translated to the dominance of regional centers over money centers in the West.

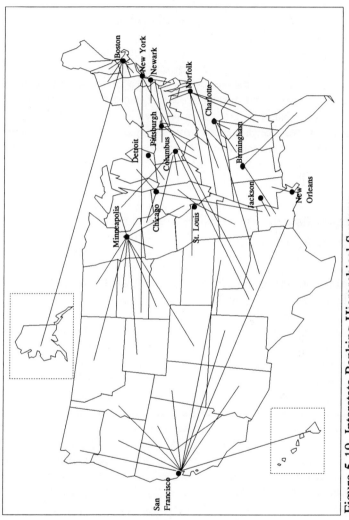

Figure 5.19 Interstate Banking Hierarchical Systems

DOMINANCE OF THE LARGEST METROPOLITAN
AREAS IN THE U.S. METROPOLITAN BANKING

Wheeler and Dillon (1985) and Wheeler and Zhou (1994) have shown the close relationship between bank deposits and the population of metropolitan areas, and corporate activities among the largest metropolitan areas. Such · concentration indicates the largest metropolitan areas to be the most important location for banking related activities. This study will further show that intermetropolitan banking and interstate banking are exceptionally intense in the largest metropolitan areas. Such an active role in banking is reflected in both the extraordinary concentration of banking resources in the largest metropolitan areas and in the dominance of large centers in the banking field.

Concentration of Banking Resources
and Banking Ownership

In 1990, the largest 100 metropolitan areas housed 76% of the total U.S. metropolitan population. However, as of early 1991, more than 80% of deposits in the metropolitan system were located in the top 100 metropolitan areas. The percentage of banking offices in the top 100 metropolitan areas is 71%, lower than their population share. This indicates that in the largest metropolitan areas, the number of banking offices per person is fewer but the average size of banking offices is larger, compared with smaller metropolitan areas. As for intermetropolitan ownership, the largest metropolitan areas account for 90% of total out-flow of banking deposit ownership and 87% of total out-flow of banking office ownership, while receiving only 73% of inflow banking deposits and 69% of inflow banking offices. This indicates that most intermetropolitan banking ownership originates in the largest metropolitan areas, and that, though they have at the same time been the largest receivers of these external ownership, the smaller metropolitan areas have disproportionately received a larger share of inflow of ownership than their population share.

In the bank holding and interstate banking areas, the importance of the largest metropolitan areas is more distinct. Both total deposits and banking offices controlled by bank holding companies in the top 100 metropolitan areas surpass their population share, at 83% and 78% respectively. This indicates that the largest metropolitan areas are the most important for bank holding activities. Of the total external ownership, 92% of deposits, or 90% of banking offices originated in the largest metropolitan areas. The shares of inflows of ownership in deposits and banking offices are 74% and 69% respectively, lower than the population share in the largest metropolitan areas. As for interstate banking holding, the top 100 metropolitan areas originate ownership for 96% of deposits and 94% of banking offices that are located in other states. At the same time, they are the receivers of 79% of inflow of deposits and 75% of banking offices.

Clearly, the largest metropolitan areas are the most important players in the banking field. They house the largest banks and control the largest share of banking resources. In addition, they export banking control to smaller metropolitan areas and nonmetropolitan areas through branching and intermetropolitan and interstate bank holding. They are also the largest receivers of external banking ownership. Such importance appears to increase from branch to bank holding, to interstate bank holding.

Spearman correlation coefficients between metropolitan population and other banking aggregates are generally supportive of the above results. The strongest coefficients occur for the largest metropolitan areas. For example, the coefficients between metropolitan population and total metropolitan deposits, and between population and metropolitan deposits held by bank holding companies are 0.84 and 0.85 respectively for the top 100 metropolitan areas, but only 0.32 and 0.47 respectively for metropolitan areas ranked from 101 to 200, and 0.46 and 0.39 respectively for metropolitan areas ranked from 201 to 335. In other words, the close relationship between population and banking resources, as revealed by Wheeler and Dillon (1985), and Wheeler and Zhou (1994), only exists within the largest metropolitan areas.

Although there generally exists a close relationship between metropolitan population and banking resources for the top metropolitan areas, the relationship is poorly described by the widely used rank-size rule, as illustrated by Figure 5.20. Although the curves demonstrate a slightly downward tendency, the generally poor associations between the variables depicted would prevent a well-fitting rank-size relationship. As a matter of fact, the resource distribution among top metropolitan areas is quite uneven. Figure 5.21 shows that when moving down the hierarchy, the total banking resource possession is characterized by distinct ups and downs. In terms of resources held between metropolitan areas, uneven distribution becomes even more apparent (Figures 5.22 and 5.23).

The Spearman correlation coefficients between various banking resources for the largest metropolitan areas are given in Table 5.16. Strong associations are found between total deposits and deposits held by bank holding companies (0.90), and between out-flow to other states and out-flow to the same state under bank holding (0.74). These indicate that in general, centers with large bank resources are more likely to become major bank holding centers, and those centers that generate intrastate intermetropolitan bank holding are also likely to generate much interstate bank holding. In contrast, the coefficient between out-flow and inflow under the branch system is 0.27, between intrastate out-flow and intrastate inflow it is -0.04, and between out-of-state out-flow and out-of-state inflow under bank holding it is -0.03. These coefficients indicate that in general centers that generate substantial out-flow banking ownership are less likely to be major receivers of inflow ownership. In other words, there is a clear division of labor in the banking field in that command/control functions are highly distinguished between different centers. Table 5.17 lists the top 15 metropolitan areas in out-flow and inflow for different categories. In each of the categories, there are only four to five metropolitan areas that appear in both the out-flow and inflow groups. Other centers have clear-cut functions as either a generator or receiver of external ownership. Figures 5.24 through 5.26 further illustrate that the distinction between generators and receivers of external ownership becomes more prominent when outflow and inflow changes from the branch system (Figure 5.24) to the bank holding system (Figure 5.25) and to interstate bank holding (Figure 5.26). In other words, the command/control function becomes more and more concentrated in a small number of centers when decision-making moves to a higher corporate level, and/or concerns a large geographic area.

Table 5.16 Spearman Correlation Coefficients Between Out-Flow and Inflow Banking Ownership

	MSA	HMSA	OUT	IN	HOI	HII	HOUT	HIN
MSA	1.00							
HMSA	0.90	1.00						
OUT	0.50	0.47	1.00					
IN	0.19	0.14	0.27	1.00				
HOI	0.43	0.51	0.28	-0.10	1.00			
HII	0.17	0.20	0.16	0.38	-0.12	1.00		
HOUT	0.48	0.55	0.25	-0.13	0.74	-0.19	1.00	
HIN	0.42	0.47	0.24	0.26	-0.06	-0.15	-0.03	1.00

MSA: Total deposits in a metropolitan area.
HMSA: Total deposits held by BHCs in a metropolitan area.
OUT: Out-flow of ownership from a metropolitan area under branch system.
IN: Inflow of ownership from other metropolitan areas under branch system.
HOI: Out-flow from a metropolitan area to metropolitan areas in the same state under BHC system.
HII: Inflow to a metropolitan area from metropolitan areas of the same state under BHC system.
HOUT: Out-flow from a metropolitan area to out-of-state metropolitan areas under BHC system.
HIN: Inflow to a metropolitan are from out-of-state metropolitan areas under BHC system.

Table 5.17 Ranking Top 15 Out-flow and Inflow Metropolitan Centers

Rank	Bank System		BHC System	
	Out-flow	Inflow	Out-flow	Inflow
1	San Francisco	Nassau	San Francisco	Washington DC
2	New York	Los Angeles	Charlotte	Houston
3	Los Angeles	Anaheim	New York	Dallas
4	Dallas	Oakland	Boston	Los Angeles
5	Newark	Philadelphia	Los Angeles	Wilmington
6	Richmond	San Diego	Norfolk	Atlanta
7	Buffalo	San Jose	Columbus	Phoenix
8	Washington DC	Baltimore	Atlanta	Tampa
9	Pittsburgh	New York	Minneapolis	Philadelphia
10	Jacksonville	Washington DC	Middlesex	Baltimore
11	Tampa	Middlesex	Pittsburgh	Oakland
12	Miami	Monmouth	Baltimore	Louisville
13	Boston	Buffalo	Detroit	Seattle
14	Hartford	Houston	Richmond	Hartford
15	Seattle	Sacramento	Cleveland	Miami

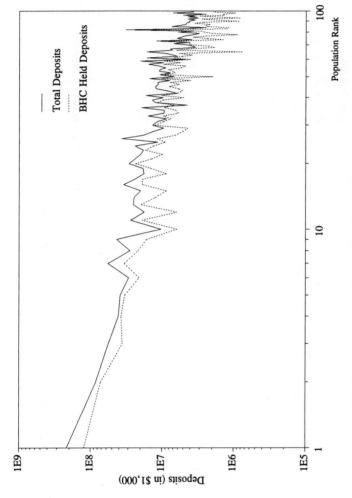

Figure 5.20 Rank Size Rule: Deposits in the Top 100 Metropolitan Areas

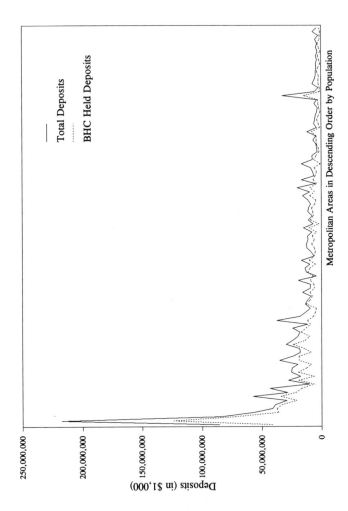

Figure 5.21 Deposits in the Top 100 Metropolitan Areas

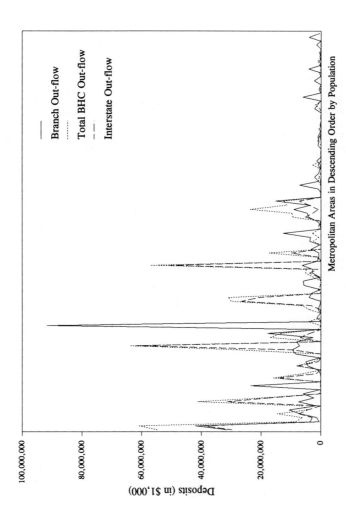

Branch Out-flow

Total BHC Out-flow

Interstate Out-flow

Deposits (in $1,000)

100,000,000

80,000,000

60,000,000

40,000,000

20,000,000

0

Metropolitan Areas in Descending Order by Population

Figure 5.22 Out-flows in the Top 100 Metropolitan Areas

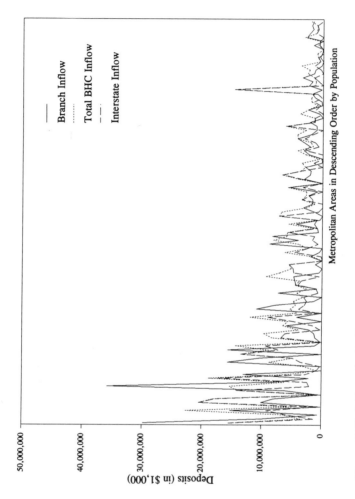

Figure 5.23 Inflows in the Top 100 Metropolitan Areas

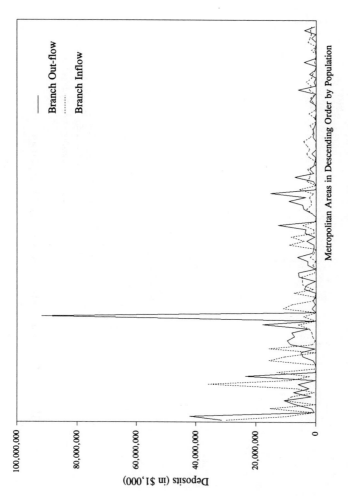

Figure 5.24 Branch Out-flow and Inflow in the Top 100 Metropolitan Areas

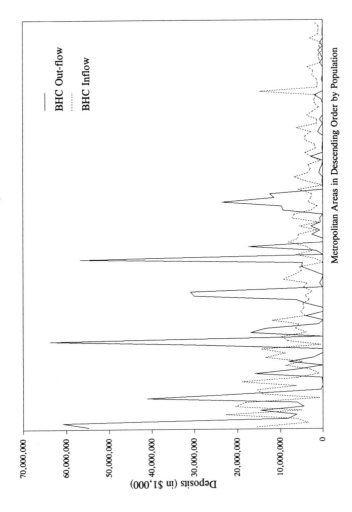

Figure 5.25 BHC Out-flow and Inflow in the Top 100 Metropolitan Areas

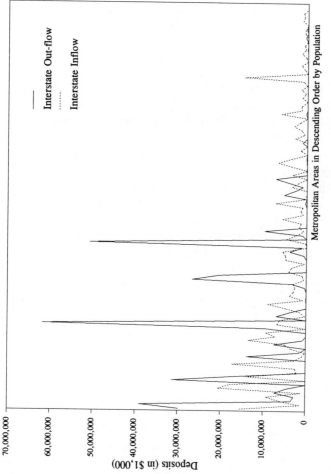

Figure 5. 26 Interstate Out-flow and Inflow in the Top 100 Metropolitan Areas

Interstate Banking Command/Control Centers

In addition to the ill-fit rank size rule relationship illustrated in Figure 5.20, this study also uses a conventional spatial interaction model, in which the dependent variable is the amount of interstate deposit holdings; the independent variables are airline distance between origins and destinations, population, and total deposits at origins and destinations. Despite variants of the model being experimented with, the overall goodness-of-fit of the model is poor: the R-squared is lower than 0.20 for all models. The great majority of the parameter estimates, especially those for interstate banking origins and destinations, are statistically insignificant.

The poor result in applying conventional geographic models in interstate banking is not a surprise. Until the early 1990s, interstate banking laws were engineered by separate state legislative actions. As a result, a hodgepodge of unrelated state banking laws carves out an uneven banking space. Spatial complementarity, transferability and competing destinations are not determined by market forces. Rather, they are determined by artificial barriers to banking. The conventional approach has been unable to separate this crucial factor from other factors and has derived corporate dominance from the sheer size of metropolitan areas. Poor modeling necessarily results.

The state of Illinois is a typical example. Illinois has a tradition of highly restrictive regulations on multilocation banking. Until 1960, Illinois had a unit banking system, in which banking operations were conducted only at the head office and no branching was permitted. In 1967, banks were allowed to establish additional offices, but only confined within a certain distance of the head office. Up to the early 1990s, in-state branching was limited to banks' host counties and contiguous counties with a limitation on the number of branches. In terms of in-state bank holding, for a long time, the state was divided into several regions and in-state bank holding was only allowed in neighboring regions. As a result of the long time regulatory restrictions, the Illinois banking system is highly fragmented. Figure 5.27 reveals the hierarchical structures under the bank system and bank holding system for Illinois. Both systems contain separate clusters, indicating a fragmented structure (Nystuen and Dacey 1961; Taaffe and Gauthier 1973). Fragmented banking structure and a weak regional

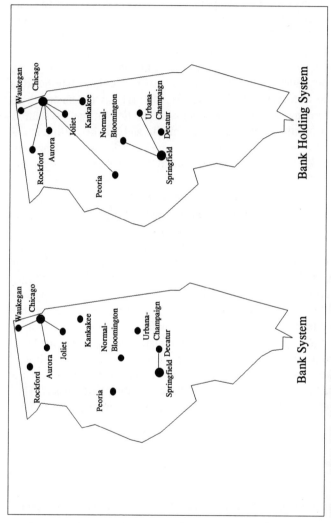

Figure 5.27 Illinois Banking Hierarchies

economy contribute directly to Chicago's weak position in interstate banking. Chicago has the third largest population, the 6th largest deposits held by banks, and the 7th largest deposits held by bank holding companies in the metropolitan system. However, Chicago ranks only 21 in out-of-state deposit holdings and only 302 in C value. Ironically, Illinois allowed banking entry from other states in the mid-1980s. As a result, many areas in Illinois were accessible to out-of-state bank holding companies but were not accessible to Chicago bank holding companies. Figure 5.28 shows 3 of the 15 interstate banking hierarchical systems revealed previously. Illinois is divided among three regional banking centers: The dominance of the Chicago system is confined to northern Illinois, while middle and southern Illinois are dominated by Michigan and Missouri banks. Such a spatial fragmentation in banking can hardly be reflected in the conventional geographic models.

In order to determine interstate banking command/control centers, Wheeler's C value approach is used. Forty seven command and control centers have been identified due to their positive C values. 274 centers have negative C values and hence are target centers. The twenty six largest command and control centers control over 90% of out-of-state held deposits (Table 5.18). All these 26 interstate banking command/control centers are among the top 100 largest metropolitan areas in terms of the size of population. However, a crucial factor that contributes to their command/control position in interstate banking is that they are the headquarter locations of major interstate banking bank holding companies, as discussed in the next subsection. In addition, most of these 26 largest interstate banking command/control centers are located in the interstate acquiring states, as identified earlier. This would directly contribute to the interstate banking function of their host state.

Bank Holding Companies in Interstate Banking

Bank holding companies are the organizational basis for interstate banking. The spatial pattern of interstate banking is largely a manifestation of the organizational structure of major bank holding companies. Recent decades have seen the rise of regional banking companies and the decline of money center banks (Kohn 1991;

Table 5.18 The Twenty-Six Largest Command and Control Centers in Interstate Banking Defined by the C Value (Unit of the C Value: millions of dollars)

Metropolis	C Value	Metropolis	C Value
San Francisco, CA	54962	Greensboro, NC	5194
Charlotte, NC	50510	Atlanta, GA	3434
New York, NY	37617	Birmingham, AL	2754
Boston, MA	31359	Baltimore, MD	2633
Norfolk, VA	26010	Newark, NJ	2198
Columbus OH	19560	Albany, NY	1806
Los Angeles, CA	14504	St. Louis, MO	1271
Minneapolis, MN	12941	Grand Rapids, MI	1055
Pittsburgh, PA	9592	New Orleans, LA	1026
Middlesex, NJ	9084	Wichita, KS	484
Richmond, VA	7118	Milwaukee, WI	254
Cleveland, OH	6598	Honolulu, HI	94
Detroit, MI	6093	Youngstown, OH	76

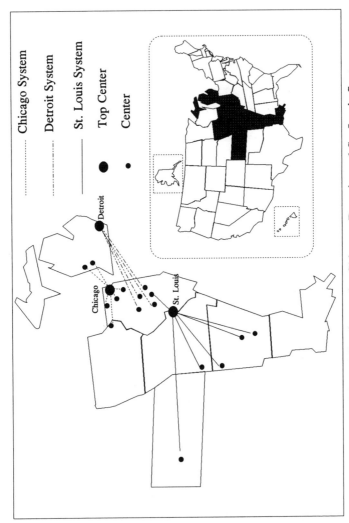

Figure 5.28   A Division of Territory: the Chicago, Detroit, and St. Louis Systems

Kamerschen 1992). Money center banks refer to the large banking firms headquartered in New York and Chicago that historically dominated the U.S. banking industry. In recent decades, Chicago banks have suffered from a weak regional economy, compounded by highly restrictive banking regulation in Illinois. New York banks have been hard hit in the LDC debt crisis (Rogers 1993). As a result, money center banks' dominance has dramatically decreased. Unlike money center banks, regional banking companies had limited overseas operations and were less affected by the LDC debt crisis. Many host states of regional banking companies have less restrictions on multilocation banking. In addition, regional banking compacts that developed during the early stage of interstate banking, shielded regional banking companies against competition from money center banks (Rose 1989). Many companies rose to regional dominance through regional banking. These companies are frequently referred to as the "regionals" and "super-regionals."

In order to analyze the role of different bank holding companies in interstate banking, metropolitan multistate bank holding companies are categorized into four groups: money center banks are bank holding companies that are headquartered in the money centers of New York and Chicago, and which are among the top 100 in assets. Super-regionals are bank holding companies in nonmoney centers and are among the top 50 in assets. Regionals are bank holding companies that are in nonmoney centers and which rank from 51 to 100 in assets. Small banks constitute the rest of the bank holding companies. Results pertaining to interstate banking patterns of bank holding companies can be summarized in three areas.

First, Regionals and super-regionals are the dominant force in interstate banking. Among different multistate bank holding companies, the shares of the regionals and super-regionals in out-of-state holdings are disproportionately higher than their shares in total assets (Table 5.19). Regionals and super-regionals as a group account for almost 90% of out-of-state held banking assets. Therefore, regionals and super-regionals are the most important factors in current interstate banking. The dominance in interstate banking by regionals and super-regionals has changed their attitude toward competition from money center banking firms. Since the early 1990s, most regionals and super-regionals have abandoned the regional approach and turned to support nationwide interstate banking.

Table 5.19 Asset Distribution Among Bank Groups

	Share in Total Assets of MSBHCs* (%)	Share in Total Out-of-State Held Assets by MSBHCs* (%)
Money Center	31.8	6.5
Super-regional	38.4	63.1
Regional	23.4	26.0
Small	4.8	3.2
Total**	98.4	98.8

*: MSBHCs: Multistate banking holding companies
**: The totals do not round up to 100%. The remainder is held by MSBHCs in nonmetropolitan areas.

Second, the distribution of multistate bank holding companies contributes directly to the formation of command/control centers in the metropolitan system. Over half the metropolitan multistate bank holding companies are headquartered in the 26 largest command/control centers, controlling over 90% of out-of-state held assets. Fifteen multistate bank holding companies are particularly important in interstate banking (Table 5.20). Each of these bank holding companies has over 10 billion dollars in out-of-state held assets. Together, they account for three quarters of out-of-state held assets in the nation. They are the basis of seven out of the top 10 command/control centers.

Finally, spatial networks of the major multistate bank holding companies shape the geographical patterns of interstate banking. Figure 5.29 shows examples of the subsidiary networks of major New York banks and super-regionals. As examples of regionals, Figure 5.30 shows the networks of important Missouri multistate bank holding companies. All these corporate networks are highly comparable with the command/control fields of these bank holding companies' home states, as revealed previously. Apparently, as Clarke (1985) and Ross (1992) suggested, it is the large multistate bank holding companies that lay down the organization foundation for the command/control fields. In comparison, most small bank holding companies have very limited corporate networks. The average number of states where bank holding companies have operations is 2.3 for small multistate bank holding companies. Most of these networks extend to neighboring states.

LATEST DEVELOPMENT OF U.S. INTERSTATE BANKING

Previous data analyses have largely been based on the information contained in the 1991 *Deposits* and *Income tapes*. Since the early 1990s, important changes have taken place in the U.S. banking industry, which has brought appreciable alterations to the patterns illustrated above. The fundamental forces of change have mainly come from the dynamics of the large bank holding companies, both money center banks and regionals and super-regionals. Table 5.21 highlights selected major U.S. banking mergers and acquisitions in recent years in which all merging and acquiring banking holding companies were among the 100 largest in the nation. A few points can be made

Table 5.20 Major Multistate Bank Holding Companies

Bank Holding Companies	Number of Member Banks	Interstate Asset Holding ($ Bil.)	States of Operation
Citicorp, New York	12	12.8	AZ DE FL MD NV NY SD ME CA
Chase Manhattan Corp., New York	9	14.0	CA DE AZ FL MD NY OH
BankAmerica Corp., San Francisco	10	403.6	AZ CA ID NM OR NV TX
First Interstate Bancorp, Los Angeles	21	31.8	AK AZ CA CO ID MT NV OK OR TX UT WA WY
First Bank System, Inc., Minneapolis	11	12.9	CO IL MN MT ND SD WI
First Union Corp., Charlotte	8	50.3	DC FL GA MD NC SC TN VA
Fleet Financial Group, Inc., Providence	13	25.9	CT ME NH NY RI

Table 5.20 Major Multistate Bank Holding Companies (Cont'd)

Bank Holding Companies	Number of Member Banks	Interstate Asset Holding ($ Bil.)	States of Operation
KeyCorp, Albany	11	30.5	AK ID ME NY OR UT WA WY
National City Corp., Cleveland	19	11.4	IN KY OH
National Westminster Bancorp, Inc. Jersey City	2	18.2	NJ NY
NationsBank Corp., Charlotte	8	122.4	DC FL GA KY MD NC SC TN
Norwest Holding Co., Minneapolis	82	23.8	AZ CO IA IL IN MN MT ND NE SD WI WY
Shawmut National Corp., Hartford	3	14.2	CT MA NH
State Street Boston Corp., Boston	3	13.4	CA CT MA
Wachovia Corp., Winston-Salem	4	12.9	DE GA NC

Table 5.21 Selective U.S. Banking Acquisitions in Recent Years

Acquiring or Merging Company	Headquarters Location	Acquired or Merged Company	Headquarters Location	New Company	New Company Location	Time of Completion & Type of Acquisition
BankAmerica	San Francisco	Security Pacific	Los Angeles	BankAmerica	San Francisco	1992, Merger
BankAmerica	San Francisco	Continental Illinois Corp.	Chicago	BankAmerica	San Francisco	1994, Acquisition
Bank of Boston Corp.	Boston	Baybanks, Inc.	Boston	Bank of Boston Corp.	Boston	1996, Acquisition
Chemical Banking Corp.	New York	Manufactures Hanover Corp.	New York	Chemical Banking Corp.	New York	1993, Merger
Chase Manhattan Corp.	New York	Chemical Banking Corp.	New York	Chase Manhattan Corp.	New York	1996, Merger
Charter One Financial Inc.	Cleveland	First Nationwide Bank	Detroit	Charter One Financial Inc.	Cleveland	1996, Acquisition of 21 branches
CoreStates Financial Corp.	Philadelphia	Meridian Bancorp	Reading, PA	CoreStates Financial Corp.	Philadelphia	1996, Merger

Table 5.21 Selective U.S. Banking Acquisitions in Recent Years (Cont'd)

Acquiring or Merging Company	Headquarters Location	Acquired or Merged Company	Headquarters Location	New Company	New Company Location	Time of Completion & Type of Acquisition
Firstar	Milwaukee	American Bancorporation	St. Paul	Firstar	Milwaukee	1996, Acquisition
First Chicago Corp.	Chicago	NBD Bancorp, Inc.	Detroit	First Chicago NBD Corp.	Chicago	1996, Merger
First of America Bank Corp.	Kalamazoo	Security Bancorp, Inc.	Southgate, MI	First of America Bank Corp.	Kalamazoo	1992, Merger
First Union Corp.	Charlotte	First Fidelity Bancorp	Newark, NJ	First Union Corp.	Charlotte	1996, Merger
Fleet Financial Group. Inc.	Providence, RI	Shawmut Corp.	Boston	Fleet Financial Group. Inc.	Providence, RI	1997, Merger
Harris Bankcorp, Inc.	Chicago	Suburban Bancorp.	Chicago	Harris Bankcorp, Inc.	Chicago	1994, Acquisition
KeyCorp.	Albany	Security Trust	Cleveland	KeyCorp	Cleveland	1991, Merger

Table 5.21 Selective U.S. Banking Acquisitions in Recent Years (Cont'd)

Acquiring or Merging Company	Headquarters Location	Acquired or Merged Company	Headquarters Location	New Company	New Company Location	Time of Completion & Type of Acquisition
NationsBank	Charlotte	Bank South	Atlanta	NationsBank	Charlotte	1995, merger
NationsBank	Charlotte	Boatmen's Bancshares,	St. Louis	NationsBank	Charlotte	1997, Merger
Northern Trust Corp.	Chicago	Bent Tree Bank	Dallas	Northern Trust Corp.	Chicago	1996, Acquisition
PNC Bank Corp.	Pittsburgh	Midlandtic Corp.	Edison, NJ	PNC Bank Corp.	Pittsburgh	1995, Merger
Southern National Corp.	Lumberton, NC	BB&T Financial Corp.	Winston-Salem	Southern National Corp.	Winston-Salem	1995, Merger
Union Bancorp	San Francisco	Bank of Boston's Corporate Trust business	Boston	Union Bancorp	San Francisco	1995, Acquisition
U.S. Bancorp	Portland, OR	West One Bancorp	Boise	U.S. Bancorp	Portland, OR	1995, Merger
Wells Fargo & Company	San Francisco	First Interstate Bancorp	Los Angeles	Wells Fargo & Company	San Francisco	1996, Merger

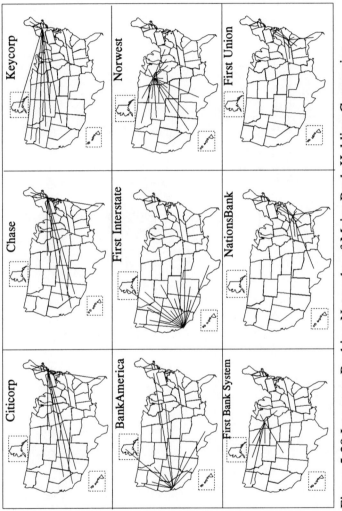

Figure 5.29 Interstate Banking Networks of Major Bank Holding Companies

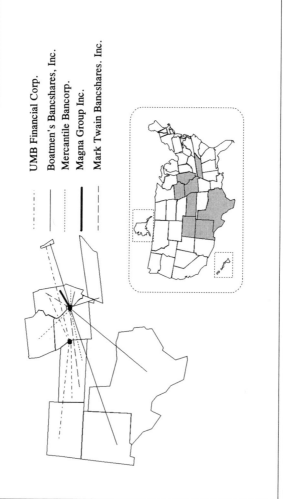

Figure 5.30 Interstate Banking Networks of Major Missouri Bank Holding Companies

concerning the latest wave of major banking restructuring. First, it is noted that a few major mergers involved money center banks, such as Chemical Banking Corp.'s merger with Manufactures Hanover Corp., Chase Manhattan Corp.'s merger with Chemical Banking Corp., First Chicago Corp.'s merger with the NBD Bancorp, Inc., and Harris Bancorp. and Northern Trust Corp.'s expansion. These moves seemed to represent a combat by money center banks amid the severe competition from regional and super-regional banking companies. Money center banks' strategies are either to combine forces with other money center banks, or to consolidate banking resources with regional banking firms. These tactics not only strengthened the position of traditionally dominant banking companies, but also eliminated some of the competitors in the regional market. These mergers will subsequently strengthen the position of money centers as the nation's first tier of financial centers.

Second, super-regional banking firms are consolidating their position by absorbing other regional or especially major regional banking firms. The examples include the NationsBank's merger with Bank South, Bank of Boston Corp.'s merger the Baybanks, Inc., Fleet Financial Group, Inc.'s merger with Shawmut Corp., First Union's merger with First Fidelity, BankAmerica's merger with Security Pacific, and Wells Fargo's merger with First Interstate. As a result, these super-regional banking firms will be in an advantageous position in their continuous competition with money center banks. Super-regional banking centers such as Boston, Providence, Charlotte, and San Francisco will also maintain their regional dominance, if not moving up the place banking hierarchy. The 1980s banking revolution has seen the emergence of numerous regional and super-regional banking firms. Since the early 1990s, consolidations among new and powerful regional banking firms have dominated the several regional banking markets.

Third, until the early 1990s, the middle section of the country seemed to be shielded from invasion of money center banks and coastal super-regional banking firms. This allowed the emergence of regional and super-regional banking firms such as the First Bank System in Minneapolis and Boatmen's Bancshares in St. Louis. Minneapolis and St. Louis consequently became the major regional banking centers in the Midwest. Toward the mid 1990s, the barrier to banking in the Midwest seems to have finally collapsed, partly due to the 1994

Interstate Banking and Interstate Branching Efficiency Act. In fact, immediately after the passage of the 1994 legislation, NationsBank began to pursue possible banking entry into the Midwest, a move that was only made legal by the 1994 legislation, since the several Midwestern states including Missouri and Minnesota only allowed regional reciprocal interstate banking. NationsBank's merger with the largest Midwestern banking firm Boatmen's Bancshares opened a new space in interstate banking competition for the Midwestern market. Boatmen's Bancshares was ranked 26th in 1996 corporate assets in the country. Other major Midwestern banking firms such as Mercantile, UMB, Commerce, etc., are all among the top 100 banking firms in the nation and possess considerable banking resources and markets. Therefore, these second tier or third tier banking firms would potentially be acquisition targets for the first tier banking firms. In the foreseeable future, the first tier banking firms will extend their banking networks into the middle section of the country and the Midwestern cities will eventually be incorporated into a national banking place hierarchy centered on money centers and super-regional banking centers on the East and West coasts.

A BRIEF SUMMARY OF FINDINGS

This chapter has revealed a process in which a fragmented U.S. corporate banking landscape is in a transition to an integrated spatial system. The fragmentation of the U.S. banking landscape is reflected in the isolation among states under the branch system, and the spatially skewed and regionally oriented interstate banking activities under the bank holding system up to the early 1990s. The transition toward an integrated spatial banking pattern has mainly been the result of banking holding ownership. Such a holding system is important in both improving connectivity in states with strong unit banking and limited branch banking traditions, and establishing connections among states. Furthermore, the new developments in interstate banking since the early 1990s seem to have been concentrated on consolidation of major regional banking companies and have ushered in cross regional consolidation. In addition, the uneven development in interstate banking in the metropolitan system has resulted in distinct command/control structures at the metropolitan, and state levels. Finally, the dominance of the largest metropolitan areas in banking activities is associated with various types of banking corporate ownership. This is reflected in the increase of dominance of the largest metropolitan areas in the entire metropolitan system from the branch system to the bank holding system.

NOTES

1. Density is the ratio of total number of entries to the total number of cells in a matrix.

2. A digraph is a graph in which entries have directions.

3. There are eight variables since both the amount of deposits and the number of offices are used.

4. Suppose places A and B. A holds 10 million dollars of deposits in B while B holds 5 million dollars of deposits in A. The pairwise C-value for A is therefore 5 million dollars while that for B is negative 5 million dollars.

VI

Banking Efficiency Estimation

This chapter addresses the third research question: what is the operational efficiency of the U.S. metropolitan banking system? Specifically how does the operational efficiency of a banking firm change with banking spatial structure and its hierarchical position in metropolitan system? The first section discusses a cost function and its specification in estimations. The second section discusses some definitions of efficiency indicators in allocative efficiency. The third section discusses data, variables and estimation procedures. The fourth section presents the estimation results. The last section summarizes the major findings of the chapter.

DUALITY THEORY AND COST FUNCTION

The conventional firm efficiency assessment literature evaluates firm performance using certain indicators constructed with parameters from either production functions or cost functions. Thus, a starting point for banking firm performance evaluation is to estimate production or cost functions of banking firms in order to obtain estimates of parameters. Although both approaches are applicable to certain economic activities, a cost function approach has the advantage that for a banking firm that generally provides multiple products (services), a cost function can explicitly include multiple outputs in the estimation. Therefore, the cost function approach is adopted in this research. The validity of a cost function in describing a production process is proven by duality theory (Shephard 1953). According to duality theory, a production process can be equally described by a maximum production function or a minimum cost function. A cost function of this nature must possess the regularity requirement specified by Diewert (1971), i.e., real value and nondecreasing in outputs, nondecreasing and weak concavity in input prices. The importance of duality theory is that information on the specific form of the production function is not necessary in order to obtain a minimum cost function. Thus, a cost function can be used to define an underlying production process with the same significance as a production function as long as the regularity condition is met. A cost function defined in such a context states that the total cost is a function of outputs and input prices. The estimations within this research will adopt a flexible form of cost function: the translog cost function.

Suppose a general form of cost function is given as follows:

$$C = C(Q_1, Q_2 \ldots Q_n, P_1, P_2 \ldots P_m) \tag{6.1}$$

where C is the total cost of a banking firm's operation, Q's are n banking outputs (services), and P's are the prices for m factors of production used in the banking operation. A translog form of the cost function given in (6.1) is $logC = C(logQ, logP)$. Specifically:

$$logC = \alpha_0 + \sum_{i=1}^{n} \alpha_i logQ_i + \sum_{t=1}^{m} \alpha_t logP_t$$

$$+ \frac{1}{2}\sum_{i=1}^{n}\sum_{j=1}^{n} \beta_{ij} logQ_i logQ_j \tag{6.2}$$

$$+ \frac{1}{2}\sum_{t=1}^{m}\sum_{h=1}^{m} \beta_{th} logP_t logP_h + \sum_{i=1}^{n}\sum_{t=1}^{m} \gamma_{it} logQ_i logP_t + e_c$$

where e_c is an error term. For a production process, when all input prices incur the same percentage increase, the total cost will also increase by that percentage. Such a characteristic requires a cost function exhibit linear homogeneity in input prices. That is, the following conditions must be met in a cost function:

$$\sum_{t}^{m} \alpha_t = 1; \quad \sum_{t}^{m} \beta_{th} logP_t = 0; \quad \sum_{i}^{n} \gamma_{it} logQ_i = 0 \qquad (6.3)$$

The partial derivatives of the total cost function (6.2) with respect to input prices are given as

$$S_t = \frac{\partial logC}{\partial logP_t} = \alpha_t + \beta_{tt} logP_t + \sum_{i=1}^{n} \gamma_{it} logY_i + \sum_{h=1}^{m} \gamma_{th} logP_h + e_s^t \qquad (6.4)$$

Equation 6.4 gives the factor shares in total cost. Since there are m inputs used in production, there are m such cost share functions. Statistical estimation of a cost function can be conducted using one or some of these factor share relations, or the original total cost function. More often, the total cost function (6.2) and factor share equations (6.4) are used to simultaneously estimate parameters in order to increase estimation efficiency by increasing available information. In estimations that use cross-sectional data, there may exist contemporaneous correlations between disturbances of the cost function and cost share functions for a simultaneous estimation. Thus, Zellner's seemingly unrelated regression technique is used. This is a generalized regression in simultaneous equation estimations, which uses the covariance matrix of residuals from different equations to approximate a covariance matrix of disturbances as weights in the generalized regression (Zellner 1962). This approach can be iteratively used in an estimation until convergence occurs (the covariance is small enough to meet the specified magnitude). It has been proved (Greene 1993) that the estimates are the same as the full information maximum likelihood estimates and are asymptotically unbiased. Since the sum of the cost share equations is equal to one, one of the share equations must be dropped to avoid singularity. In a full information maximum likelihood estimation, the estimates are not affected by which share equation is dropped (Greene 1993). The conditions in (6.3) can be met by placing linear constraints on parameters. In addition, since some of the same parameters occur in different equations, across equation constraints on parameters are required.

The flexible form is not the only possible specification. The alternatives include various neoclassical specifications such as the Cobb-Douglas, homogeneous, homothetic, or constant returns to scale forms. These different forms can be easily obtained by using linear restrictions on the cost function parameters. For example, for a Cobb-Douglas form, the conditions $\beta_{ij}=0$, $i=1,...,n$; $j=1,...n$; $\beta_{th}=0$, $t=1,...,m$; $h=1,...,m$; $\gamma_{it}=0$, $i=1,...,n$; $t=1,...,m$ must be met. For a homothetic function, the conditions $\gamma_{it}=0$, $i=1,...n$; $t=1,...,m$ must be met. For a function homogeneous of degree α, the conditions are $\beta_{ij}=0$, $i=1,...,n$; $j=1,...,n$; $\gamma_{it}=0$, $i=1,...,n$; $t=1,...,m$; $\Sigma\alpha_i=\alpha$, $i=1,...,n$. When $\alpha=1$ is specified, a linear homogeneous function is obtained. These linear restrictions are subject to statistical test. Therefore, various neoclassical specifications on the production function can then be tested.

EFFICIENCY INDICATORS

The concept of efficiency can be defined in two broad senses: technical efficiency and allocative efficiency (Morrison 1993). Technical efficiency refers to the fact that given resources generate the maximum output. Allocative efficiency refers to the fact that production occurs at the lowest possible cost, i.e., the optimal input combinations. In a production space, the concept of technical efficiency can be illustrated with an isoquant of a given level of product. For the same isoquant, if the level of product for one firm is higher than that of another firm, the latter firm is said to be technically inefficient. A given level of product can be produced with different combinations of inputs, represented by different points on an isoquant. Only at the point where the marginal rate of transformation and price ratio are the same can the production be said to be efficient. Other points on the isoquant are said to experience allocative inefficiency. Technical inefficiency is a result of not using the best technology available. Allocative efficiency results from failing to respond to market signals. Both inefficiencies will result in the inefficient use of resources. Allocative efficiency can be measured by using indicators associated with total factor productivity, economies of scale, and economies of scope. Technical efficiency can theoretically be measured with capacity utilization in a cost function framework. However, since the estimation of capacity use is usually conducted by estimating the short-run cost function, this contradicts the underlying assumptions for a long-run cost function estimated in this research. Thus, technical efficiency will not be estimated in this research.

Total Factor Productivity

The total factor productivity (TFP) is a measure of efficiency associated with those factors that are not explicitly expressed in a production function and, thus, cannot be accounted for by function parameters. In his original study, Solow (1957) used TFP to measure changes in production over time, attributed generally to changes in technology. This has precipitated much research within econometrics on changes in productivity over time. However, Solow also suggested that TFP may consist of the effect of different economic structures. Sato and Nono (1983) define TFP as including technological changes, economies of scale, and changes in economic structure. Denny and Fuss (1983) generalized TFP into a spatial context in which TFP measures differences in economic structure that exist between places but are not explicitly reflected in a production function.

This research adopts the TFP approach to measure the effects of various structural factors. Conceptually, structural factors, which are not explicitly included in a banking firm production function, include the spatial configuration of banking networks, the metropolitan hierarchical positions of banking operation sites, BHC affiliation status, branch/unit structure, and the regional environment, as well as other factors. Therefore, it is conceivable that TFP actually measures a combination of all these factors. Assume that these different factors are separable. Thus, if all other factors are controlled for except one, TFP measures would be quite close to the effect of the factor that remains uncontrolled for. Aivazian, *et al.* (1987) partly adopted this approach in estimating a production function for natural gas transmissions. Instead of treating TFP as economies of scale, they introduced a homogeneous parameter to capture the economies of scale. They then treated the estimated TFP as the effect of structural changes. Chapter 3 has discussed the difficulties of estimating the effects of factors that are not readily observable and quantifiable. The TFP approach provides a possible solution. This approach will be a major strategy in this research to estimate the effects of various structural differences, especially concerning spatial structure and the metropolitan hierarchical position of banking operation location.

The measurement of TFP is basically an accounting procedure. Assume a translog production function $LogQ=f(LogL, LogK, R)$, where L and K represent inputs used in production. In a banking context, L may represent all real resources while K represents all financial resources. R represents a structural factor that is left uncontrolled for. The translog function can be written as

$$LogQ=\alpha_0+\sum_{X=L}^{K}\alpha_X logX+1/2\sum_{X=L}^{K}\sum_{X=L}^{K}\beta_{XX}logXLogX$$
$$+\gamma_R R+1/2\sum_{X=L}^{K}\gamma_{RX}RlogX+\gamma_{RR}R^2/2+Rm \qquad (6.5)$$

where α, β, and γ are parameters and Rm is a remainder. The above production function is a Taylor expansion at point $LogL=LogK=1$.

Suppose two points in R: R_1 and R_2. First, expand at point 1 and evaluate the function at point 2; then expand at point 2 and evaluate the function at point 1. Finding the differential between the two values, there exists:

$$LogQ_2-logQ_1=1/2\sum_{X=L}^{K}(f'_{2.X}+f'_{1.X})(X_2-X_1)$$
$$+1/4(f''_{2.LK}-f''_{1.LK})(LogL_2-LogL_1)(LogK_2-LogK_1) \qquad (6.6)$$
$$+\delta+1/2(Rm.1-Rm.2)$$

where f' and f'' are the first and second order partial derivatives, $Rm.1$ and $Rm.2$ are remainders, and δ is a composite value which contains total differentials in all terms that involve R. Specifically:

$$\delta = 1/2 \sum_{X=L}^{K} (f'_{2.R} + f'_{1.R})(R_2 - R_1)$$

$$+ 1/4 \sum_{X=L}^{K} (f''_{2.RX} - f''_{1.RX})(R_2 - R_1)(logX_2 - logX_1) \qquad (6.7)$$

In this general form of the production function, δ is a measure of total factor productivity. According to Denny and Fuss (1983), if R is a temporal variable, δ is an intertemporal index number; if R is a spatial variable, δ is then an interspatial index number. Based on the same principle, if R is a structural variable such as the spatial configuration of a banking network, δ can be similarly labelled an interstructural index. In (6.6), assuming that remainders are zero and rearranging the terms, the TFP δ can be expressed as

$$\delta = (LogQ_2 - logQ_1) - 1/2 \sum_{X=L}^{K} (f'_{2.X} + f'_{1.X})(X_2 - X_1) \qquad (6.8)$$

$$- 1/4(f''_{2.LK} - f''_{1.LK})(LogL_2 - LogL_1)(LogK_2 - LogK_1)$$

Since this research estimates banking firms' cost functions, the TFP will be measured with a cost diminution, a concept similar to δ. For the translog cost function in (6.2) there exists

$$-\delta_Q = \delta_C = log C_2 - Log C_1 - 1/2 \sum_i^n (\alpha_{i2} + \alpha_{i1})(Log Q_{i2} - Log Q_{i1}$$

$$-1/2 \sum_{t=1}^m (\alpha_{t2} + \alpha_{t1})(log P_{t2} - Log Q_{t1})$$

$$-1/2 \sum_i^n \sum_j^n (\beta_{ij2} - \beta_{ij1})(Log Q_{i2} - Log Qsubi1)(Log Q_{j2} - Log Q_{j1})$$

$$-1/2 \sum_t^m \sum_h^m (\beta_{th2} - \beta_{th1})(Log P_{t2} - Log P_{t1})(Log P_{h2} - Log_{h1})$$

$$-1/2 \sum_i^n \sum_t^m (\gamma_{it2} - \gamma_{it1})(Log Q_{i2} - Log Q_{i1})(Log P_{t2} - Log P_{t1})$$

$$(6.9)$$

where δ_Q is TFP from the production function while δ_C is cost diminution from the cost function. This is a cost function version of TFP measurement. Information on TFP and information on cost diminution is equivalent if the regularity of a cost function is met.

The accounting procedure (6.9) essentially requires two cost functions, C_1 and C_2. The function C_2 acts as a baseline in order to measure the magnitude of variations in C_1. In this research, the cost function for the entire U.S. metropolitan system is used as such a baseline. The cost functions in controlling groups as specified in Table 6.1 are in turn treated as function C_1. The strategy is first to estimate cost functions to obtain parameter estimates. These estimates are then substituted into (6.9) to calculate cost diminution, i.e., TFP.

Economies of Scale and Scope

Economies of scale are the efficiencies associated with the size of operation. From the cost side, economies of scale are said to exist if for a certain percent increase in outputs, cost increases less than that percent. Using a translog cost function, an indicator of economies of scale, E_c, can be defined as:

$$E_c = \sum_{i=1}^{n} \frac{\partial logC}{\partial logQ_i} = \sum_{i=1}^{m} (\alpha_i + \sum_{j=1}^{m} \beta_{ij} logQ_j + \sum_{t=1}^{t} \gamma_{it} logP_t)$$

(6.10)

In practice, when $E_c < 1$, economies of scale are said to exist. When $E_c > 1$, diseconomies of scale are said to exist. When $E_c = 1$, there are constant returns to scale. This standard of comparison is unduly constrained in that for a flexible, nonhomogeneous function, the sum of cost elasticities are not independent of the point of evaluation. If one chooses to evaluate each model at small data points, economies of scale indicators can all be less than one for a well-behaved cost function. To avoid possible subjectivity associated with this standard, this research evaluates economies of scale at the sample mean. The emphasis is not on a less-than-one indicator but on the comparison of the magnitude of indicators between different models. In other words, each model is treated as a representation of an average banking firm in a designated comparison group. A smaller magnitude of indicator indicates a better performance in terms of the economies of scale. This standard of comparison essentially looks at average firm performance in an economies of scale continuum.

Economies of scope are said to exist if different products or services can be produced at a lower cost within the same firm than the sum of the cost when producing them in separate firms. That is, $C(Y) < \sum C_i(Y_i)$. Panzar and Willig (1977) defined the concept of economies of scope precisely as $\partial^2 C / \partial Y_i \partial Y_j < 0$. An approximate test of this condition, using estimates of a translog cost function, is shown to be

$$\alpha_i \alpha_j + \beta_{ij} < 0$$

(6.11)

The second term on the left-hand side is the parameter of the interaction term between two outputs, while the first term is the product of the first-order parameters of the two outputs. A well-behaved cost function (concave toward the origin) will necessarily have positive first-order parameters with respect to outputs. Thus, the product of the two first-order terms is positive. If the joint effect of the outputs on cost is negative and the magnitude of the parameter is sufficiently large, the above condition is met. Intuitively, this means that a cost curve shifts downward due to the presence of another output.

Financial Spread

Two financial spreads are defined in this research. The first is the market efficiency gap, defined as the gap between overall marginal cost and average income. Assume an efficient banking firm adjusts its last unit of input to the point where the marginal cost is equal to the market price of its product, represented here by average income. The gap then is a measure of how close a firm's marginal cost is to its price. A small gap is usually taken as a measure of efficiency since this indicates the firm can provide service at a lower cost compared to price (Blair and Kaserman 1985; Saunders and Walter 1994). The other financial spread, the gap between average income and average cost, is a measure of profitability. The two financial gaps are compared to analyze if high profitability is a result of efficient services, a typical textbook situation. The marginal cost is not usually available. It must be derived from the estimated cost function with

$$\frac{\partial C}{\partial Q} = (\sum_i^n \frac{dLogC}{dLogQ_i}) * \frac{C}{Q}$$

(6.12)

The term in parenthesis can be obtained by taking derivatives in an estimated cost function with respect to different outputs. This is an estimated cost elasticity of output.

In addition to the above indicators, the Allen partial elasticities of substitution will also be calculated. These elasticities of substitution not only indicate the substitutability between input pairs and review the shape of isoquants (i.e., curvature in a production space), but also help determine if the cost function meets the regularity requirement specified by Diewert (1971) so that the shape of the cost function can be determined. Allen partial elasticities can be calculated using the following formulas

$$\Omega_{th} = (\beta_{th} + S_t S_h) / S_t S_h$$

$$\Omega_{tt} = (\beta_{tt} + S_t (S_t - 1)) / S_t^2$$

(6.12)

where Ω's are the Allen elasticities of substitution, S' are factor shares, and β's are parameters for relevant factor price terms in (6.2). Caves and Christensen (1980) show that a negative value for the self-substitution terms on the Allen elasticity of substitution matrix diagonal indicates the regularity of the cost function. Only if this requirement is met, can the shape of a cost function at the estimation point be specified. Thus, the production function and cost function behave consistently. In other words, the analysis can be based on production function theory.

DATA, VARIABLES, AND ESTIMATION PROCEDURES

The data used in estimation are extracted from the *Income tape*. In estimating cost functions, total operational expenses are used as costs. Five categories of inputs are used. These include expenses in labor, capital (including rental, premises), transaction accounts (including demand deposits, negotiable order of withdrawal (NOW) accounts, and other deposits), nontransaction accounts (including time and saving deposits such as money market accounts, certificate of deposits, saving accounts, and other time deposits), and the rest of the inputs (major components are a variety of security categories of liability). The number of employees in a bank is used as a proxy for the amount of labor. Although distinction between management staff members and other ordinary banking clerks would be preferred, limitation in data prevents this approach. The price of labor services is simply found by dividing the number of banking workers into the cost of total salaries and other benefits. Capital is approximated by using the expenditure on rental and premises. Following the convention of Murphy and White (1983), the price of capital is found by total expenditure on capital divided by total deposits. Transaction accounts and nontransaction accounts are available on the *Income tape*. The interest rates for either are obtained by dividing the total amount of each account into the total interest expenditures on each account. The rest of the inputs are obtained by subtracting total deposits and equity from total liability. The price of this category of inputs is obtained by using the total expenditure minus expenditures on deposits, capital, and salaries and benefits, divided by the dollar value of inputs in this category.

Four outputs are used. These include commercial loans, real estate holdings, consumer loans and other asset holdings such as holdings in securities. Real estate holdings include both real estate investment and holdings of real estate capital. Given four outputs and five inputs used in estimation, the simultaneous equations specified in (6.2) and (6.4) contain five equations including one cost function and four factor-share functions. The total number of parameters to be estimated is 55, including the intercept. Appendix C lists the independent variables and equations in the simultaneous estimation used in this research.

The estimation is conducted following two principles. The first is to separate effects of as many factors as possible. That is accomplished by putting banks into different categories according to their operating environments or conditions. This is especially important in estimating TFP. These different conditions are (1) whether or not banks are affiliated with bank holding companies; (2) whether or not banks are branch banks and unit banks; (3) whether or not banks are operating in major metropolitan areas; and (4) the region in which the banks are located. In condition (3), a bank headquartered in a particular metropolitan area may not have its entire operation in that metropolis due to intermetropolitan branching. Therefore, this condition can only control for the operating environment of unit banks. For branch banks, this is only an approximation of their operating environment, though the majority of branches of a banking firm tend to locate in the same metropolitan area where the head office is located.

The second principle used in estimation is to obtain a sufficient sample size for each model. Iterative seemingly unrelated regression generates parameter estimates that are asymptotically unbiased. This requires reasonably large sample sizes in order to reduce estimation bias. This determines that the number of categories of models must be confined within a certain limit.

The estimations are conducted in nine series. The three major series are regional: North, South, and West as defined by the U.S. census. Within each region, banks are grouped according to whether or not they are affiliated with BHCs. Within each group (with and without BHC affiliations), banks are further divided into two types: branching or unitary. In each type, the distinction is made according to whether banks are headquartered in the top 100 metropolitan areas (large), in other metropolitan areas ranking from 101 to 200 (medium), or the rest (small ranking from 201 to 335). Series Four divides banks according to bank company affiliation, branch/unitary division, and metropolitan hierarchy. Series Five divides banks according to the branch/unitary division and metropolitan hierarchy. Series Four and Five are therefore basically special cases of the first three series. They are designed as supplements to the first three series since some categories in the these series do not have enough observations. Series Six is used to estimate the model according to spatial orientation/cluster as discussed in Chapter V. Series Seven groups banks according to their network characteristics such as how many branches and in how many metropolitan areas the banking firms are operating. Series Eight is the bank holding company model. This is used to estimate cost functions for bank holding companies, as a comparison between bank holding companies and branch banks. Series Nine controls for bank size. Banks are grouped into three size classes based on the size categories given on the *Income tape* (Large banks with assets valued at more than 300 million dollars; Medium banks with assets between 100 and 300 million dollars; and small banks with assets of less than 100 million dollars). In certain respects, this category overlaps with others. For example, branch banks with BHC affiliations and a large metropolitan location tend to be large in size. In addition, banks without BHC affiliations and with a small metropolitan location tend to be small in size. Category Nine is designed to supplement other models. These series and the factors controlled for in these model categories are illustrated in Table 6.1.

Table 6.1 Model Series in Estimation and the Factors Controlled

Series	Factors Controlled				
	Region	Hierarchy	BHC	Branch	Network
One	yes	yes	yes	yes	no
Two	yes	yes	yes	yes	no
Three	yes	yes	yes	yes	no
Four	no	yes	yes	yes	no
Five	no	yes	no	yes	no
Six	no	no	no	yes	yes
Seven	no	no	no	yes	yes
Eight	yes	no	yes	no	no
Nine	-	-	-	-	-

Series One: the North Model
Series Two: the South Model
Series Three: the West Model
Series Four: the BHC/non-BHC Model
Series Five: the Branch/Unit Model
Series Six: the Spatial Orientation Model
Series Seven: the Network Model
Series Eight: the Bank Holding Company Model
Series Nine: the Size Model
-: irrelevant

ESTIMATION RESULTS

Model Specification Tests

Cost functions with and without neoclassical assumptions are tested by introducing appropriate restrictions on parameters. Appropriate measures from both are used to construct an F test statistic (Greene 1993). Comparisons are made between the unconstrained model and models with constraints of the Cobb-Douglas form, homothetic function, homogeneous function, and the function of constant returns to scale. The R squared terms from constrained and unconstrained models are used to construct such a statistic. A sample of such a test is given in Table 6.2 which lists the F values for various comparison groups with branch/unitary division. In all situations, the F value is large enough to decisively reject the null hypothesis at the 0.01 significance level. Thus, an unconstrained, non-neoclassical model is preferred.

Normality is tested with the Shapiro-Wilk statistic (when models contain less than 2000 observations) and the Kolmogorov test (models with more than 2000 observations). In all situations, the null hypothesis that the residuals are normally distributed is rejected at the 0.05 level. However, for models with large sample sizes (approximately more than 120), the null hypothesis cannot be rejected at the 0.1 level. A visual examination of the residual plots against the independent variables reveals that in most models, residuals are reasonably evenly distributed along the zero axis. Even in models with less than 100 observations, such behavior is still retained. Therefore, it may be concluded that the residuals in most models with large sample sizes are normally distributed.

A major problem with the data set is the existence of substantial collinearity. Using the data set for the branch/unit category, the eigenvalues of the first principal components are found to be over 20 and the condition indices are greater than 50 in most models. Considering that there are 54 independent variables in the models, an eigenvalue over 20 indicates a high redundancy among independent variables. This is to be expected due to the co-existence of the first, second, and cross terms in the model. Pearson correlation coefficients confirm such an expectation. Strong correlation exists between the first

Table 6.2 Model Specification Test for Model Series V: Branch and Unit Banks

Model	Number of Constraints	BRANCH F	BRANCH R^2	UNIT F	UNIT R^2
Unconstrained			0.993		0.977
Homothetic	20	12.14	0.992	5.81	0.975
Homogeneous	30	218.49	0.977	132.19	0.932
Linear Homogeneous	31	211.4	0.976	127.93	0.929
Cobb-Douglas	45	163.66	0.975	2.97	0.919
Number of observations		3010		2154	

The null hypothesis can be rejected at 0.01 for all models.

and second order terms of the same variables. Cross terms also tend to strongly correlate with one or two of their component terms.

Strong collinearity will tend to increase the variance of estimates making it difficult to obtain significant estimates. In this regard, estimations in this research suffer similar problems as do most socioeconomic studies. That is, various socioeconomic variables are more or less correlated (Theil 1978; Greene 1993).

Although there is substantial collinearity, it is unreasonable to say that it is fatally detrimental to the estimations of this research. One of the major negative consequences of collinearity is the large variance of estimates and the insignificant estimates of parameters. In this research, however, all models estimated contain a substantial number of significant estimates. In fact, when the sample sizes rise above 200 observations, 70 to 80 percent of 55 estimates from the seemingly unrelated regression are usually significant at the 0.01 or 0.05 levels. This may be due to several reasons. The first is the large sample size for each model (usually over 150 observations), which may help reduce the variances of estimates. Secondly, the 55 variables in the cost function contain an enormous amount of information, and thus they help improve efficiency. In addition, the simultaneous equation estimation used contains five models. This adds additional information (e.g., four factor shares) to the model. For example, a comparison is made between the OLS and simultaneous equation estimation in branch banking operation. In a model that contains all branch banks in the metropolitan system, of the 55 estimates of the cost function, the OLS contains 33 insignificant estimates while the simultaneous equation approach contains only 15. It should be noted that the significant estimates themselves do not necessarily mean that the effects of collinearity are not detrimental. A significant estimate may still contain the effects from several closely related variables, making the interpretation of estimates difficult.

Perfect remedies to collinearity are not available. Dropping certain variables will simply destroy the cost function specification, causing other problems in estimation. Given a theoretically derived cost function, large sample size, and a multiple equation setting, the detrimental effect of collinearity is believed to be largely controlled for. What is required is extra caution in interpretation of the estimation results.

Heteroscedasticity between observations within the model does not seem to be substantial. As evidenced by the small magnitude of correlation coefficients between residuals and independent variables. In no case are the coefficients larger than 0.4. Residual plots against dependent variables also show no specific patterns indicating correlations with exogenous variables. Contemporaneous correlations between models are reduced through an iteration process where the residuals of previous runs are used to construct a covariance matrix of across model residuals, as estimates of a covariance matrix of disturbances in a generalized regression. This iteration process continues until convergence occurs as defined by a certain criterion. The default criterion in the computing facility is $1.0*10^8$.

In summary, data used in this research are not perfect in that some assumptions for regression models such as independence of the variables are not strictly observed. However, there are several reasons to believe that the detrimental effects of collinearity are more or less controlled for by increasing sample size. In addition, a model specification with a strong economic foundation may be equally important in forming a statistical model. Finally, iterative seemingly unrelated regression will increase the estimation efficiency by correcting the across-model contemporaneous correlations and by incorporating more available information in a simultaneous equation estimation.

Efficiency Estimation Results

Sixty-nine models are estimated to obtain parameter estimates, which are in turn used to calculate efficiency indicators, at the 0.1 significance level. Appendix C contains calculated performance indicators for Series One, using the North model as an example.

Three patterns are observed in most models. The first is the widely observed economies of scope. In almost every model, there exist some economies of scope. This lends support for a full service banking operation. The second pattern that is widely observed is small elasticities of substitution among various inputs. The elasticity of substitution between labor and capital is low in most cases, and in some cases, unitary. This result is surprisingly close to the Cobb-Douglas form. Most other elasticities also have small magnitudes (smaller than 2). A small elasticity of substitution among different inputs indicates that the isoquants in a production space have large curvatures. Therefore, for a given change in input price ratio, changes in input ratios brought about by input substitutions are rather limited. This finding reveals the general shape of the production space for banking firms.

Compared with generally small elasticities of substitution, the elasticity of substitution between transaction and nontransaction accounts generally show relatively large magnitudes, indicating that the two accounts are in a direct competition. In addition, the negative sign of elasticities of substitution between labor and transaction accounts and the positive sign between labor and nontransaction accounts seem to indicate the role of human labor in different kinds of deposit taking: more expensive labor would discourage transaction accounts and encourage nontransaction accounts. In other words, compared with nontransaction accounts, transaction accounts may be more labor intensive. The generally negative sign of the elasticity of substitution between capital and transaction accounts and in many situations, nontransaction accounts, indicates that the increase in deposits must be accompanied by an increase in banking facilities. This may be an indirect indication that branch operations can enhance financial resources, although not necessarily increase operating efficiency. The third uniformly observed phenomenon is that in Allen elasticity matrix the diagonal items are negative. This indicates a cost function complying with the regularity requirement specified by Diewert (1971). In other words, at the estimation points, the cost functions are well behaved. Therefore, general production/cost theories apply.

Although the above indicators show strong uniformity across models, the rest of the indicators, such as economies of scale, the total factor productivity associated with various structure characteristics, and financial spreads, are extremely diversified. Patterns are not easy to identify in some cases and do not exist at all in others. All patterns displayed exist with exceptions. The following analysis is conducted according to various indicators.

Economies of Scale. A general pattern is that banking firms do better in large metropolitan areas than in small ones. In the North and South regional series, banks in the top 100 metropolitan areas show better economies of scale performance than banks in medium-sized metropolitan areas. Banks in the latter group in turn do better than those in small-sized metropolitan areas. This pattern generally holds for banks with and without BHC affiliations, as well as for branch and unit banks. One exception is in the North where unit banks with BHC affiliations in the smallest metropolitan areas do better than those in median-sized metropolitan areas. In the West, there are not enough observations available for most of the medium- and small-sized metropolitan areas for a meaningful estimation. When putting unit banks affiliated with bank holding companies in medium- and small-sized metropolitan areas, the result shows consistency with the North and South.

Such hierarchical patterns are supported by evidence from Series Four, the division of BHC affiliation. For banks with BHC and without BHC affiliations, and for branch banks as well as unit banks, banks in large metropolitan areas are shown to be associated with relatively good performance in terms of economies of scale. An exception is unit banks with BHC affiliations, where the smallest metropolitan areas seem to offer better economies of scale performances than in medium-sized metropolitan areas. This is a similar picture to that found in the North Series. In Series Five, the previously revealed pattern holds for branch banks, but fails to hold for unit banks in the smallest metropolitan areas, which present better economies of scale performances than in the medium sized metropolitan areas. Apparently, in all cases, the pattern revealed holds except for unit banks with BHC affiliations.

The distinction in the economies of scale indicator is not clear between banks with and without BHC affiliations, nor between branch and unit banks. In addition, no clear and convincing regional patterns are discovered.

The study of economies of scale in the banking industry is always controversial. In this research, great inconsistencies exist even if regional division, BHC affiliation, and branch/unit division are controlled for. No solid evidence or consistent pattern was found to convincingly support the claim that multi-location banking through branching and bank holding can help economies of scale in banking. However, the pattern seems to be clearer when the metropolitan hierarchy is controlled for. That is, when regions, BHC affiliations, and the branch/unit division are controlled for, banks in the top metropolitan areas tend to show stronger economies of scale than their counterparts in medium and small metropolitan areas. In other words, economies of scale may be affected not only by branching and bank holding, as many economists believe, but also by specific place conditions. As major banking fields the large metropolitan areas attract a disproportionate amount of banking resources. Such resource concentration and the resultant intensive competition increases the pressure on banking firms to grow in size to strengthen their competitiveness (Kohn 1991). The large amount trading in each individual deal also calls for the rise of large banking firms. In addition, the diverse banking markets in major metropolitan areas require multiple functions and large banking organizations. Unit banks and banks without BHC affiliations also experience cost advantages associated with size, compared with their counterparts in smaller-sized metropolitan areas. This indicates that generally, banking firms in large metropolitan areas have a shallow U-shaped average cost curve, which allows banking firms to grow with limited incremental cost.

Banks in medium and small metropolitan areas face proportionately less concentration and thus a less competitive environment, compared with their counterparts in large metropolitan areas. They also face less competition from other financial institutions such as investment banks. In addition, the size of the economies in small and medium metropolitan areas requires a comparable banking size structure (Rose 1989). As a result, cost efficiency can be achieved at smaller sizes. In short, contrary to the suggestion of most economic studies, there is no single universal optimal size for banking firms located differently. The optimal size of banking firms should be a place-specific concept. Such optimal size is a result of a combination of local resource concentration, inter-firm competition, and local banking market conditions. Theoretically, an industrial cost function/curve is possible only if firms are facing similar economic geographic conditions. Pooling firms from largely different economic environments would be unlikely to lead to meaningful conclusions.

The Structural Difference Associated With the Metropolitan Hierarchy.
The structural differential associated with the metropolitan hierarchical positions of banking firms is captured by finding the TFP between a particular metropolitan model and the base model, as expressed in (6.9). A pattern emerges in that branch banks in large metropolitan areas, no matter what their BHC and regional status is, generally suffer from a negative TFP. The TFP measures are negative in most large metropolitan areas and have the tendency to turn positive or show a reduced negative magnitude when moving down the metropolitan hierarchy. Most models in the North and South support this pattern.

The West model shows a negative TFP in large metropolitan areas. Evidence from Series Four and Five, the BHC/non-BHC and branch/unit models also support this pattern. Supplementing this pattern is the tendency that in these large metropolitan areas, unit banks tend to do better than branch banks, and non-BHC banks tend to do better than BHC banks. Since branch banks and BHC banks in large metropolitan areas are generally associated with large banks, the above pattern can be interpreted to mean that large banks in large metropolitan areas generally suffer from negative externalities. This impression is reinforced by evidence from Series Nine which shows that in large metropolitan areas banks with an asset value greater than 300 million dollars have a more negative TFP than smaller banks.

A small or negative TFP in large metropolitan areas indicates that banks in large metropolitan areas have a high cost associated with the large metropolitan environment. This result is unexpectedly contradictory to the general belief that large metropolitan areas provide cost savings due to urbanization and localization economies.

A possible explanation for this finding can be found in the conventional notion of diseconomies of urbanization and/or localization. The disproportionate concentration of banking activities may have caused elements that contribute to negative externalities in large metropolitan areas. Some of these elements are measurable and others not. The measurable elements include higher wage rates, rental rates, and interest rates associated with over-concentration of banking and other economic activities. These factors have been directly introduced into the models and thus accounted for. Elements that are nonmeasurable and thus could not be accounted for by TFP may include intensive competition and resultant declining market shares for banks operating in large metropolitan areas. Such competition may come not only from within the banking industry, but also from other financial institutions that are becoming more aggressive in competing with banks. Kohn (1991) and Kamerschen (1992) attributed massive disintermediation to the aggressive expansion of various forms of investment banks including finance companies, mutual funds, and other money management companies. Both Hayes and Hubbard (1990) and Eccles and Crane (1988) discovered a concentration of investment companies in major metropolitan areas. Wheeler (1986a) also found the concentration of investment banks at the very top of the metropolitan hierarchy. Investment banks are specialized in investment in stocks, bonds, and money market instruments. Since these capital and money markets are mainly located in major metropolitan areas, the spatial concentration of investment banks in large metropolitan areas is natural. Statistical publications of different sources[1] show that 80 to 90 percent of investment institutions listed are headquartered in large metropolitan areas. Given the severe competition, the negative external environment for banks in large metropolitan areas seems to be inevitable. However, such speculation must be supported by direct evidence in further investigations.

Structural Differences Associated With Spatial and Network Structures. Measurement of the effects of spatial and branch structures on the operational performance of banking firms is conducted by measuring the TFP associated with different spatial structures and branch structures. The results generally fail to show any distinct pattern.

For models in Series Six that is designed to measure the effect of banking network structure, the estimations are conducted with branch, unit, and all banking firms separately, using the spatial structure orientations obtained in Chapter 5. The estimations are conducted for Clusters I to VI only since there are not enough observations for Cluster VII. When pooling all banks in the cluster, the unit orientation model demonstrates substantial negative TFP. This leaves the impression that restrictive branch legislation may help reduce productivity. However, the largest negative TFP occurs within the out-flow orientation. This is a direct contradiction with the conclusion that may be drawn from the previous model. By examining the unit bank models, it can be seen that unit banks in Cluster III, the unit orientation, have the worst TFP of all, a result consistent with the overall model. Unit banks with a metropolitan orientation, Cluster V, however, show much better TFP than the overall model in the same cluster. The branch model of Cluster V shows a very negative TFP. Cluster III does not have enough observations to obtain any estimate of TFP for the branch model. The pattern discovered in Cluster V also occur in Clusters I and II, the mainstream and on-site/unit orientations, where branch models show a poorer TFP than unit bank models do. It seems that although unit/on-site orientation does negatively affect the productivity of banking firms, orientations that emphasize branching may not necessarily guarantee a positive compensation. In addition, unit banks may not be the source of negative TFP. The negative effects of branch banks may be overwhelming.

For Series Seven models that include different network types, the results are also inconclusive. Banks with three or less branches and a banking field that spreads over only one metropolitan area do show the worst TFP, worst economies of scale, and the highest marginal cost. Banks with four-to-nine branches and with only one metropolitan banking field demonstrate a much better performance in terms of TFP, economies of scale, and marginal cost. However, banks with more than ten branches and one metropolitan field fail to demonstrate significantly better performance than the first group, the three-or-less branch group. Similarly, banks that operate in more than one metropolitan market fail to show significantly better performance than one-metropolitan market banks. Therefore, the conclusion that an extensive intra- and inter-metropolitan branch network would necessarily improve banking performance cannot be drawn from this research.

One possible reason for negative TFP of outflow orientation and extensive branch structure is that the effect of expansion through branching out is concealed by a model that uses only one year's cross-sectional data. A textbook production/cost function usually adjusts instantaneously, leaving no room for fixed cost in a long-term cost function. That is, moving from one equilibrium position to another in a production space is portrayed to occur instantaneously. Thus, the production or cost curve is smooth and continuous. In actuality, changes in production/cost functions reflect a long-term temporal process. The expansion of a branch network both in intra- and inter-metropolitan contexts reflects a banking firms' vision on the potential benefits of banking expansion through time. The actual adjustment may be discrete, in disequilibrium, and time-consuming. Moving from one equilibrium position to another in a production space may take years. As a result, there is always a portion of resources that does not reach equilibrium, and thus functions as fixed cost. One year's data may capture only one moment during the entire adjustment process. Therefore, negative TFP may result. Only when data are collected at two equilibrium points, can the benefits of expansion be captured. In this regard, a time series estimation seems to be more appropriate in capturing a long-term change in TFP.

Structural Differences Associated With Bank Holding Companies. The effect of BHCs on banking performance can be measured by the TFP controlling for BHC affiliations (Series One to Series Four).

Alternatively, a bank holding company cost function can be estimated and the TFP calculated and compared with branch banks without BHC affiliations (Series Eight).

Series Four shows that banks with no BHC affiliation generally have a better TFP than banks with BHC affiliations, no matter what their metropolitan hierarchical positions. Regional models (Series One to Three) reveal a weak regional variation in large- and medium-sized metropolitan areas. In the Northern models, in large- and medium-sized metropolitan areas, banks with BHC affiliations demonstrate better TFP than those without BHC affiliations. Evidence from the South shows that banks without BHC affiliations have higher TFP than banks with BHC affiliations. Patterns found in the South are partly duplicated in the West where branch banks with BHC affiliations demonstrate higher TFP than banks with BHC affiliations.

In Series Eight, banks affiliated with the same holding company are aggregated to form a BHC. Information from different BHCs is used to estimate a BHC cost function for the North and South separately (the Western model is not estimated because there are not enough observations). The Southern model shows a poor TFP while that of the North has a substantially positive TFP. The difference in TFP between the two regional models is largely in line with models of banks with BHC affiliations in these two regions.

The different TFP between banks with and without BHC affiliations is related to the issue of dissimilarity between branch bank and bank holding companies in terms of their impact on banking performance. The above discussion provides an indirect comparison which shows that the effects of a BHC and a branch bank on banking cost effectiveness may vary regionally. A direct comparison between Series Eight models and models of branch banks without BHC affiliations shows that BHCs have substantially lower economies of scale than branch banks without BHC affiliations. The comparison of TFP between the two groups shows a similar regional pattern as described above. That is, BHCs in the North have better TFP than branch banks without BHC affiliations. In the South, the opposite situation exists.

It can be speculated that such a regional pattern, though rather weak, is due to the fact that in the North, especially in the money centers, major bank holding companies have existed for a long time and therefore are more mature in bank holding company operation. A positive TFP may be attributed to the structural advantages within a bank holding company such as coordination in the operation of multiple banks by a high-order administrative center. In terms of long-term adjustment, coordination between member banks may accelerate the adjustment process for a banking firm through fund redistribution among member banks so that banking statistics for a bank holding company as a whole can always reflect the data point that is closer to the equilibrium point.

In contrast, bank holding companies, especially those "regionals" or "super-regionals" in the South, have begun rapid growth only in the most recent decade, and therefore still are in a process of adjustment toward an optimal allocative position. Consequently, the banking data is more likely to reflect a non-equilibrium position in a production space. These speculations, however, are subject to further investigation.

The above findings should be viewed with great care due to some inconsistencies discovered among comparison regions. One such inconsistency is that banks with BHC affiliations have poorer TFP than banks without BHC affiliations in northern, and small metropolitan areas. Furthermore, the statement that banks without BHC affiliations have a higher TFP than banks with BHC affiliations, can only be made with respect to branch banks in the West. For western unit banks, the opposite situation exists. In addition, a direct comparison between the BHC models and the models of branch banks without BHC affiliations, as conducted in this research, has left many factors uncontrolled for in the BHC models. As a result, the TFP in the BHC models may contain largely different information, as compared with branch bank models.

Financial Spreads. Financial spreads in this research refer specifically to the spread between average cost and average income, and the spread between marginal cost and average income. The former is a measure of profitability of banking firms while the latter is a measure of efficiency of the market in which banking firms operate. With some exceptions, a pattern emerges. The profit spread is generally larger in BHC banks than in non-BHC banks, and larger in branch banks than in unit banks. This pattern generally holds in Series Four with the exception of small metropolitan areas where branch and unit banks without BHC affiliations have slightly larger spreads than branch and unit banks with BHC affiliations. The higher profit gap for BHC banks than for non-BHC banks is also found in most models in the South and all models in the West. In addition, this pattern prevails in all models in Series Five. There exist a few exceptions. In the South, unit banks without BHC affiliations have larger spreads than unit banks with BHC affiliations in metropolitan areas, in small and medium metropolitan areas. This same pattern occurs in the North. In addition, BHC unit banks in large and medium-sized metropolitan areas in the North have a larger spread than their BHC branch counterparts. Among three regions, the West has the largest spread. The North generally has the least spread, and the South is in an intermediate situation. No particular pattern is found concerning the metropolitan hierarchy.

Larger profit spread can be caused by different combinations of income and cost, such as, low cost and high income, high cost but even higher income, and low income but even lower cost. There is no particular pattern which links particular combinations to any particular comparison groups. This is understandable since cost and price level vary with location. It is spread, rather than actual cost and income levels, that can more accurately reflect profitability.

Market efficiency is measured by the spread between marginal cost and average income. The smaller the gap, the closer the cost of the last unit product to the reward a banking firm can get. The pattern revealed for the efficiency gap is rather weak. Among all possible alignments such as the regional, hierarchical, branch/unit, and BHC affiliation, only models of the North show any regularity. That is, banks in large metropolitan areas tend to have smaller efficiency gaps than do banks in medium and small metropolitan areas. This pattern is the same across BHC/non-BHC and branch/unit divisions.

Efforts to identify the relationship between profitability and market efficiency fail to establish recognizable patterns. Such a result indicates that a large profit spread is not necessarily associated with a large or small market efficiency gap, making it difficult to conclude the relationship between the profitability and market efficiency. In the case of BHC and branch banks, it seems that high profitability is not a result of the efficient operations of banking firms. Textbook statements that firm efficiency will generate higher profits do not hold true in the context of this research. Although a non-perfect market may contribute to the inconsistency between profitability and market efficiency, a more plausible explanation is that profitability is associated with product structures that are partly reflected in the firm size. Branch banks and banks with BHC affiliations are more likely to be large firms. Large firms are likely to operate in markets that are very different from those of small firms. In Series Nine, large banks on average tend to have larger shares in real estate, personal loans, and securities holdings than do small banks. In addition, the input structures are quite different between banks of different size. For example, in terms of input shares in total cost, large banks use less labor, capital, and transaction accounts but more nontransaction accounts and securities, compared with small banks. With the rapid growth in personal loans, real estate, and capital markets, the high profits of large banks are understandable. However, this explanation must be further investigated by, examining, for example, a profit function. A profit function expresses profits as a function of output price, input price, and inputs, and thus allows a direct investigation of the relationship between profitability and the structures of products and inputs.

A BRIEF SUMMARY OF FINDINGS

The estimations in this chapter have found widespread evidence of economies of scope and scale. In addition, it has been found that the substitutability between banking inputs is rather limited. Economies of scale become stronger for banks located in large metropolitan areas than in medium and small metropolitan areas. This indicates that the concept of economies of scale is place specific. Total factor productivity associated with large banks in large metropolitan areas shows some negative effects on banking performance. The total factor productivity associated with banking holding companies seems to show a weak regional pattern. In the North, banks with BHC affiliations do better than their non-BHC counterparts. In the South, the opposite is true: banks without BHC affiliations have larger TFP gain than banks with BHC affiliations. In general, bank holding companies do better in the North than in the South. The profit spread is generally larger in banks with BHC affiliations and branch banks compared with non-BHC banks and unit banks. Western banks tend to have higher profit gaps than banks in the South and North. Northern banks have the lowest profit gap of all. The efficiency gap is not shown to be associated with the profit gap.

NOTES

1. *Mutual Funds Panorama 1992* (CDA Investment Technologies, Inc.), *Spectrum Directory of Institutions 1992* (CDA

Investment Technologies, Inc.), and *Guide to Mutual Funds 1990* (Investment Company Institute).

VII

Summary and Concluding Remarks

This research investigates three issues in the U.S. commercial banking industry in the metropolitan system. These are, the theoretical investigation of banking firm and the banking industry's conducts in a spatial context; an empirical investigation of the spatial and hierarchical structure of the banking corporate ownership of the U.S. metropolitan system; and the statistical assessment of banking performance in the U.S. metropolitan system. These three issues are logically coherent and related in that the investigation of banking operational mechanisms in a spatial context helps in understanding the internal conduct logic and motivations of banking firms and the banking industry, and the mechanism under which the spatial distribution and pattern of banking activities are formed. Such a theoretical investigation provides a conceptual foundation for understanding the spatial behavior of the banking industry and resultant corporate banking networks and performance. This chapter provides a summary of major findings with respect to these three issues, and indicates some possible directions for further investigation.

A SUMMARY OF MAJOR
FINDINGS OF THE STUDY

Findings on the Theoretical Investigation of the Spatial Mechanism of Banking Conduct

1. The theoretical investigation of banking firm conduct in a spatial context is based on a generalized banking firm production function designed in this research. This generalized functional form incorporates multi-input, multi-output, multi-stage, and multi-location

characteristics in banking firm operation. Unit bank operation and different formulations of banking firm operation can be seen as special cases of the function. This function is theoretically consistent with the neoclassical production function in that it can be theoretically specified as a neoclassical Cobb-Douglas and Constant Elasticity of Substitution form.

2. Using the generalized banking firm production function, the operation of a banking firm in a spatial context is seen as a resource allocation among alternative locations. The crucial difference between this generalized functional form and currently widely used textbook production functions is that the operation at various branch locations are explicitly present in the function, and treated as a factor of production. Thus, the conventional neoclassical substitution notion applies. The banking firm is seen as having a joint optimization at both the local and firm levels. At the local level, the local manager targets on input allocation while at the firm level there is also an allocation of branch size at alternative locations. The marginal location product is balanced by locational cost. The equilibrium firm size occurs where the last incremental increase of operations at alternative locations brings the same increase in output at all locations.

3. The branch size of banking firms is shown to be positively related to local branch marginal productivity, and the internal and external agglomeration of economies, and negatively related to the input prices. Although this only theoretically confirms intuition, this finding provides analytical arguments in support of current studies of producer services concerning their concentration in major metropolitan areas.

4. The analyses of macro-level banking conduct have revealed two factors that help determine spatial bank holding patterns. The first factor is the community utility. Banking spatial and aspatial linkages are seen as an approach in altering and improving banking community utility. The second factor is the bank holding cost associated with various banking spatial and aspatial holdings. The combination of these two factors can explain most of the geographic bank holding patterns.

Findings on the Empirical Investigation of Geographical Structure of Banking Corporate Ownership

1. Until the early 1990s, spatial banking corporate ownership under branch ownership show great fragmentation at the national level.

More than two thirds of banking assets are held on-site, leaving only one fifth to intermetropolitan connection (the remainder are connected to nonmetropolitan areas). There is no national banking hierarchy based on branch ownership. Each state forms it own branch banking network. Fifty one state and the district branch systems operate in isolation.

2. There exist variations in spatial and hierarchical structures at the state level. Variations in spatial and hierarchical structures at the state level have a strong correspondence. The Midwest, prairie, and some Mountain states mostly belong to the unit and unit/on-site spatial structure types. Many of these states developed disjointed hierarchical structure. Both East and West coast states tend to developed more externally oriented spatial structures. They tend to develop various connected hierarchical structures.

3. Banking through bank holding companies increases both intrastate and interstate connectivity between metropolitan areas. Nearly half the banking assets held by bank holding companies are used in intermetropolitan connections. More than half the banking assets under intermetropolitan holding are held across statelines. Most entries on the bank holding company ownership matrix are found to occur between metropolitan pairs that are not connected through branching. For intrastate intermetropolitan bank holding, most new entries occur in those states with unit/on-site and unit spatial structures. After these new entries are accounted for, many of these states' hierarchical structures change from disjointed to various connected structures. For interstate intermetropolitan bank holding, almost all entries occur between metropolitan pairs that are not connected through branching.

4. Three major groups of states are identified in terms of their status in interstate banking. They are characterized as interstate banking acquirers, interstate banking targets, and those inactive in interstate banking. Fifteen independent interstate hierarchical structures are identified. These hierarchical structures contain most of the metropolitan areas and generally form regionally based banking clusters.

5. The interstate banking fields are strongly skewed and regional in nature. This is reflected by the fact that all the fifteen interstate banking hierarchical structures have regional extent. The banking fields for most states are confined to adjacent or contiguous states. New York, being blocked from entering most Midwest and Southern states, can only find its banking field in the Mountain and West coast states.

6. The largest (top 100) metropolitan areas have disproportionate importance in banking corporate networks. There is over-representation of banking assets in the largest metropolitan areas. There is even stronger over-representation of out-flow ownership in the largest metropolitan areas. The over-representation of out-flow banking ownership in the largest metropolitan areas increases from branch bank owning, to intermetropolitan bank holding, to interstate bank holding. Banking command/control becomes more concentrated within a small number of metropolitan areas when the level of banking corporate decision-making increases, and the involved geographic areas become larger. There exists a clear division of labor along the metropolitan hierarchy; large metropolitan areas are the originators of branch banking, intermetropolitan bank holding, and interstate bank holding, while the role of lower hierarchical metropolitan areas is as receivers of inflow banking ownership.

7. The largest bank holding companies have played a crucial role in shaping the interstate banking pattern. The regionals and the super-regionals, in addition to money center banks, have become the dominant force in interstate banking. The geographic pattern of interstate banking is largely a manifestation of the organizational structure of major bank holding companies.

8. The latest developments in interstate banking have indicated a consolidation at the regional level among major regional banking firms. In addition, the major cross-region banking merger between NationsBank and Boatmen's Bancshares may have indicated the beginning of the midwestern banking field being incorporated into a national banking network.

Findings on Statistical Estimation of Banking Performance

1. The estimations in this research have found evidence of economies of scope. In addition, banking cost functions generally comply with the regularity requirement, indicating that at the data point the banking cost curve generally conforms to the general belief of the U-shaped curve.

2. It has been found that the substitutability between banking inputs is rather limited. Transaction and nontransaction accounts are in more direct competition. In addition, there is evidence that a branch

system has a cost advantage in deposit taking compared with a unit system.

3. Economies of scale become stronger for banks located in large metropolitan areas compared with those in medium- and small-sized metropolitan areas. This indicates that the concept of economies of scale is place specific. Evidence of economies of scale along the BHC/non-BHC and branch/unit divisions is very inconsistent.

4. Total factor productivity associated with large banks in large metropolitan areas shows negative effects on banking performance, indicating possible effects of diseconomies of urbanization, especially competition from investment banks.

5. Total factor productivity associated with bank holding companies seems to show a weak regional pattern. That is, in the North, banks with BHC affiliations do better than their non-BHC counterparts. In the South, there is a reversal: banks without BHC affiliations have larger TFP gain than banks with BHC affiliations. In general, bank holding companies do better in the North than in the South. This difference may reflect differences in bank holding development in the different regions. However, compared with branch banks without BHC affiliation, bank holding companies have much poorer economies of scale.

6. The profit spread is generally larger in banks with BHC affiliation and branch banks compared with non-BHC banks and unit banks. Western banks tend to have higher profit gaps than banks in the South and North. Northern banks have the lowest profit gap of all. However, the efficiency gap is shown to be associated with the profit gap, leading to the conclusion that high profitability is not necessarily the result of high operational efficiency. Compared with the poor association between profitability and market efficiency, the product structure and input structure may be more relevant factors in explaining profitability.

7. Results concerning the effects of spatial and network structures on banking performances are rather inconclusive. No solid evidence is found to convincingly support the claim that geographic expansion may contribute to banking performance by improving the cost effectiveness of banking firms.

CONCLUDING REMARKS

Pierce (1991a) described banking history as a process of conflict between private firms trying to pursue individual economic advantage and government that is established to protect public interests, whatever these are defined to be. This conflict is intertwined with the conflicts among different levels of public authority. These conflicts clearly have their spatial dimension. The theoretical and empirical investigations in this research help elucidate this spatial dimension of the conflict of interests between communities.

Banking firms use space as one dimension in pursuing their individual interests of either profit optimization or utility maximization. These private goals lead banks to view differently the issue of spatial movements of banking resources, depending upon the competitive positions of banks in particular areas. A banking firm's competitive position is determined by its productivity when there is an incremental use of resources located in other locations. This productivity is indicated by the marginal productivity for banking firms. The productivity helps determine the comparative advantage of banking firms as related to competitors. This comparative advantage in turn determines the optimal magnitudes of various resource uses and therefore the optimal combination of various resources, located at various locations. The realization of such an optimal combination of resources relies on both economic and political means. This gives the opportunity for regulatory intervention to define the degree of spatial mobility of banking resources in order to maintain banking firms' comparative advantage within a certain area. Thus, economic interests provide a basis for the political interests of local communities. In other words, private business interests intertwine with the politics that are designed to protect certain groups of business interests against others.

For a country like the United States, local banking communities have been seen to rely on political means to protect or advance their private interests. This is reflected in geographic barriers to banking, existing either at the state or regional level. The spatial variations of these regulatory barriers to banking are a reflection of the uneven development of different local banking industries. The corporate banking landscape is therefore a result of spatial resource allocation via spatial political power allocation. The spatial fragmentation of corporate banking networks under the branch system, and the skewed and highly regional interstate banking under the bank holding system, as revealed in this research, are the result of these two closely intertwined mechanisms that shape the corporate banking landscape. The impacts of spatial expansion, as conditioned by resource allocation and political power allocation, on banking firm performance are theoretically clear but empirically elusive. This research has found no solid evidence showing that a spatially extended firm has a low operational cost. On the contrary, extended spatial structure is found to work against branch banks with various branch structures and BHC banks, as evidenced by their negative structural TFP. However, operating with less efficiency does not prevent branch and BHC banks from having higher profitability compared with unit and non-BHC banks. This fact, in conjunction with the evidence that market efficiency may not have a direct relationship to high profitability, indicates that the effect of banking expansion on banking performance may be a much more complicated issue than the conventional efficiency oriented approach in treating banking performances can explain.

The conventional efficiency approach focuses on banking cost effectiveness associated with various structural variables such as size, types of ownership, and branch/unit structure. Although banking cost is important, it may submerge other more salient factors that serve as motivation for banking spatial expansion. These other factors include access to a large geographic market and resultant diversification and a larger market share. These latter factors may be more important to banking firms in securing a high profit level than low cost operations. When benefits from these factors surpass the negative effects derived from high costs associated with structural variables, banking expansion results. In other words, spatial elements may be more important to profit earnings than to cost effectiveness. Thus, a profit function approach, in conjunction with a cost function approach, may be more appropriate, though the issue of data availability is more challenging.

Although it has failed to find connections between spatial structure and operational cost, this research has found that locational elements do play a role in effecting banking cost through economies of scale. Economies of scale has been a study topic in the banking literature for a long time. Controversy exists concerning whether banking services have economies of scale. The findings presented in this research generally reveal that banking firms in various comparison groups conform to the conventional notion of a U-shaped cost curve. This indicates that as far as total banking operational cost is concerned, there will be an optimal operational size at which cost is a minimum. Therefore, any drastic deviation from optimal size may not necessarily have a positive effect on banking costs. More important is the finding that economies of scale are place specific. The external environment affects banking operations. This indicates that banking regulation concerning market entry should also be place specific. A merger and acquisition in a large metropolitan area should be treated differently from one in a small metropolitan area. The Herfindal index currently used by antitrust authorities in assessing the effect of banking consolidation is generally based on market shares of banking firms, ignoring spatial variations in optimal size. Adopting a uniform standard in regulating banking consolidation may therefore hinder banking consolidation in large metropolitan areas, which would potentially reduce operational costs. Therefore, locationally specific guidelines for banking consolidation seem to be more appropriate.

The study of the U.S. banking industry is a rich field. This is so not only because the banking industry is a crucial component of the national economy, but also due to the rapid development in the U.S. banking industry in the most recent twenty years. With the latest banking laws in place, the U.S. banking industry is finally in a position to move into a fully integrated national banking system. The subsequent impacts on the national economy, local communities, and individuals as banking customers and banking employees are too tremendous to ignore. Banking researchers in different fields have made a great deal of progress in advancing understanding of banking activities. This research is a preliminary effort to bring together location theory/the regional science tradition, the corporate geography tradition, and the industry performance assessment tradition, in analyzing banking as a spatial phenomenon. It seeks to offer a geographic analysis of the U.S. banking industry in which the theoretical, empirical, and statistical elements are reasonably balanced. The research is only a first step in this direction. Several suggestions can be made for future research.

The first concerns the scope of the banking industry under investigation. Banking as a type of economic activity is no longer monopolized by the banking industry. Various nonbank financial institutions and commercial firms have invaded banking fields in competition with the banking industry. These include money market mutual funds that absorb funds by selling shares and issuing checking accounts, and automobile producers and retail chains that issue various personal loans. Competition from saving & loan institutions is also strongly felt by commercial banks. This means that a study of bank operations reflects only a segment of the entire body of banking activities. In terms of banking spatial behaviors, competitors from different fields should be included in theoretical and empirical analysis in order to fully account for the cause/effect of corporate banking expansion.

A second suggestion concerns the scope of industries involved. Banking activities are only a portion of the economy. The interactions between banks and their customers are also important in understanding the spatial behavior of banking firms, in addition to competition between banking firms. The economy in a locale is fundamental in determining the needs and kinds of banking activities. A complete analysis should account for interaction between the banking industry and other economic sectors.

The third research suggestion concerns the level of aggregation. This research focuses on the nationwide aggregate place network based on the corporate operational network. Individual banking firm networks and the banking network of particular places submerge national aggregate metropolitan banking networks. Research can be furthered by investigating individual banks and individual cities or regions to account for variations associated with banks as well as places. These individual units are the ultimate building blocks of the aggregate corporate banking place network and thus should not be left out of investigation.

The fourth suggestion concerns the types of models used in investigations. The current industrial performance study overwhelmingly focuses on cost effectiveness. In light of the fact that this research has failed to find evidence linking spatial and network structures of banking firms to their cost effectiveness, it may be concluded that the cost reduction may not be the direct result of or motivation for banking expansion. Therefore, other approaches may be necessary, in conjunction with the cost function approach, in banking performance investigations. These include the profit function and revenue function approaches. These different functions contain different performance indicators and thus provide a new angle from which to view the effect of spatial and network structure.

The final suggestion concerns the construction of spatial corporate banking networks. This research has constructed spatial corporate banking connections using deposit information. This approach should be supplemented by information that reflects different aspects of banking connections. These other aspects include loan production offices, ATM operations, and correspondent banking. These activities are part of banking operations that link places. A complete picture of the corporate banking landscape cannot be drawn without incorporating them into investigations.

Appendix A

A PROOF OF σ

To see σ, taking the derivative of $\partial f/\partial D$ with respect to D results in:

$$\frac{\partial^2 f}{\partial D^2} = \frac{\partial^2 f}{\partial L \partial D}\frac{dL}{dD} + \frac{\partial f}{\partial L}\frac{d^2 L}{dD^2} + \frac{\partial^2 f}{\partial I \partial D}\frac{dI}{dD} + \frac{\partial f}{\partial I}\frac{d^2 I}{dD^2}$$

(A1)

Let $h(L,I) = \partial f/\partial L$. Therefore,

$$\frac{\partial^2 f}{\partial L \partial D} = \frac{\partial h}{\partial D} = \frac{\partial h}{\partial L}\frac{\partial L}{\partial D} + \frac{\partial h}{\partial I}\frac{\partial I}{\partial D}$$

$$= \frac{\partial^2 f}{\partial L^2}\frac{\partial L}{\partial D} + \frac{\partial^2 f}{\partial L \partial I}\frac{\partial I}{\partial D}$$

(A2)

Similarly,

$$\frac{\partial^2 f}{\partial I \partial D} = \frac{\partial^2 f}{\partial I^2}\frac{\partial I}{\partial D} + \frac{\partial^2 f}{\partial I \partial L}\frac{\partial L}{\partial D}$$

(A3)

Notice,

$$\frac{\partial^2 f}{\partial L \partial I} = \frac{\partial^2 f}{\partial I \partial L}$$

Substituting (A2) and (A3) into (A1) yields:

$$\frac{\partial^2 f}{\partial D^2} = \frac{\partial^2 f}{\partial L \partial I}\left(\frac{\partial I}{\partial D}\frac{dL}{dD} + \frac{\partial L}{\partial D}\frac{dI}{dD}\right)$$

$$+ \frac{\partial^2 f}{\partial L^2}\frac{\partial L}{\partial D}\frac{dL}{dD} + \frac{\partial f}{\partial L}\frac{d^2 L}{dD^2} \qquad (A4)$$

$$+ \frac{\partial^2 f}{\partial I^2}\frac{\partial I}{\partial D}\frac{dI}{dD} + \frac{\partial f}{\partial I}\frac{d^2 I}{dD^2}$$

In (A4), the first line is positive, the second and third lines are negative. Thus, the condition that satisfies $\partial^2 f/\partial D^2 < 0$ is: $0 < \partial^2 f/\partial L \partial I < -(\theta + \phi)/\Omega$, where

$$\Omega = \frac{\partial I}{\partial D}\frac{dL}{dD} + \frac{\partial L}{\partial D}\frac{dI}{dD}$$

$$\theta = \frac{\partial^2 f}{\partial L^2}\frac{\partial L}{\partial D}\frac{dL}{dD} + \frac{\partial f}{\partial L}\frac{d^2 L}{dD^2} \qquad (A5)$$

$$\Phi = \frac{\partial^2 f}{\partial I^2}\frac{\partial I}{\partial D}\frac{dI}{dD} + \frac{\partial f}{\partial I}\frac{d^2 I}{dD^2}$$

Appendix B

METHODOLOGY OF DEVELOPING
A HIERARCHY TYPOLOGY

The hierarchical structure disclosed previously is seen as a graph. These graphs with different characteristics are used to extract information to construct three indices: the index of network hierarchy, the index of network centrality, and the degree of network components. The typology of hierarchical structure is constructed based on these indices.

The index of network hierarchy is defined as the ratio of sum of an individual hierarchical index within a network to the maximum possible value for such a sum in a network. The individual index of hierarchy of a place is defined as the cumulative inflow degrees of itself and of all its subordinate members. For example, in the hierarchical digraph (graph with directions) of the Alabama branch banking network (Figure B.1), there are two metropolitan areas that are directly subordinate to Montgomery. Thus, the inflow degree for Montgomery is 2. Seven metropolitan areas are directly subordinate to Birmingham. The inflow degree for Birmingham is seven. It is defined that vertices at the extremes of a path have zero value for the index of hierarchy. The index of hierarchy of Birmingham is therefore the sum of its own inflow degree and inflow degree of its subordinate, Montgomery. Specifically, the index of hierarchy for Montgomery is 2 and index of hierarchy for Birmingham is 9.

The concept of cumulative inflow degree is consistent with the Transitivity Principle in that for a particular center, its subordinates' subordinates are also subordinate to it. Thus, the inflow degrees of its subordinates carry the information of cumulative subordination from the next lower order centers. In other words, a cumulative inflow degree reflects the hierarchical position in a network for a particular center. From a graph point of view, a connected hierarchical graph is minimally connected. The shape of such a network may take two extremes: a chain or a star. The maximum cumulative inflow degrees

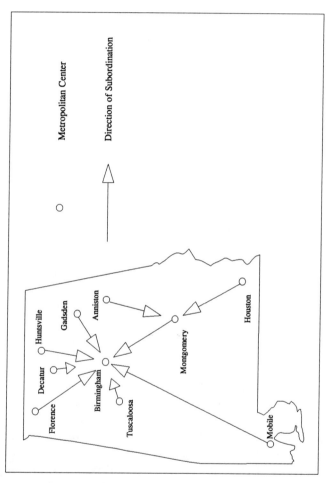

B.1 Branch Banking Network: Alabama

for the system can be proved to be $I_0 = v(v-1)/2$, where I_0 is the maximum cumulative inflow degree, and v is the number of connected vertices for a given network. Suppose the actual cumulative inflow degree in a network is I. The index of network hierarchy is then $H = I/I_0$ where H is denoted as the Index of Network Hierarchy. It can be shown that the network is a chain when $H = 1$, and a star when $H = 2/v$. If H is between 1 and $2/v$, the network is a tree. From a chain, to a tree, to a star, the layers of hierarchy decrease when the number of vertices is given. Thus for a minimally connected digraph, the higher the index of network hierarchy is, the more layers of hierarchy the system has. For a completely disjoined hierarchical structure where no hierarchical linkages exist between places, $H = 0$.

The index of network centrality is defined as the ratio of the number of non-end positioned vertices to the maximum possible number of non-end positioned vertices in a network. That is $T = v_n/(v-2)$, where T is index of centrality and v_n is number of non-end positioned vertices. A connected network is star shaped when $T = 1/(v-2)$, a chain when $T = 1$, and a tree when $1/(v-2) < T < 1$. For a star hierarchical digraph, the network is centered on a single center. When T increases, the centrality of networks decrease. When $T = 0$, no non-end positioned vertices exist. This is a null graph. Although both hierarchical and centrality indices reflect the degree of hierarchy of a hierarchical network, the index of hierarchy is a more direct measure of hierarchy while the index of centrality is an indirect measure. Only a first-order term of v exists in the formulas for the index of centrality. Therefore it is more sensitive to the size of a network. Both indices are used to accommodate different sensitivity brought about by networks of different size.

The degree of components, P, is defined as the ratio of the number of vertices (v) to the number of components (m) in a graph, i.e., $P = v/m$. When a graph is connected (in other words, a whole piece), $m = 1$ and $P = v$. For a null graph, $m = v$, and $P = 1$. When the graph is disjoined, $1 < P < v$. The degree of components measures the coherence of a hierarchical system.

After these three raw indices for hierarchical networks are constructed, they must be compared with a certain standard or the benchmark to make classification possible. The standard is determined in the following two steps. First, take the indices of a star-shaped network as the benchmark. This is so because the star shape is the least hierarchical and most central. Deviation from such a benchmark would necessarily indicate more a hierarchical nature and less centrality. For each raw index of hierarchy or centrality, multiply the index with an index obtained for a star network, using the same number of vertices in that system. For example, the actual index of hierarchy is 0.2444 for a system of 10 metropolitan areas. A star network with 10 vertices has an index of hierarchy 0.2. The converted index of hierarchy is therefore 1.222. Mathematically, the converted index of network hierarchy is

$$H_c = \frac{\dfrac{I}{\dfrac{v(v-1)}{2}}}{\dfrac{2}{v}} = \frac{I}{v-1}$$

and the converted index of network centrality is

$$T_c = \frac{\dfrac{c_m}{v-2}}{\dfrac{1}{v-2}} = c_m$$

which is simply the number of non-end positioned vertices. These are called the converted indices of network hierarchy and centrality.

Secondly, some benchmark is necessary to determine the scale of the converted indices. This is a highly arbitrary task. There are few objective criterion which the magnitude of the concerted indices can be judged upon. This study uses a threshold approach. For the index of network hierarchy, a system of at least three vertices is necessary in order to distinguish between a star and a chain. The concerted index of network hierarchy for a three vertice network chain is 1.5. Thus, if the converted index of hierarchy for a network is greater than 1.5, the network is said to be more hierarchical. For the index of centrality, a system of at least four vertices is necessary in order to be more than singlely central. A four vertice chain has a converted index of centrality of 2. Thus, if any converted index of centrality is greater than 2, the system is said to be less central or more hierarchical. Using these benchmarks and converted indices, the hierarchical networks can be classified into three major groups and seven basic types, as describe in Chapter V.

Appendix C

DEFINITIONS OF VARIABLES

Variable	Definition
LESTATE	Log of real estate investment
LCLOAN	Log of industrial and commercial loans
LPLOAN	Log of personal loans
LOTHER	Log of all other outputs
LPAY	Log of average salaries and benefits
LRATEC	Log of rental rates on capital
LRATEDEP	Log of interest rates on transaction accounts
LRATETERM	Log of interest rates on nontransaction accounts
LRATEREST	Log of rates on the rest of the inputs
SQESTATE	Square of log of real estate investment
SQCLOAN	Square of log of industrial and commercial loans
SQPLOAN	Square of log of personal loans
SQOTHER	Square of log of all other outputs
SQPAY	Square of log of average salaries and benefits
SQRATEC	Square of log of rental rates on capital
SQRATEDP	Square of log of interest rates on transaction accounts
SQRATERM	Square of log of interest rates on nontransaction accounts
SQRATERE	Square of log of rates on the rest of the inputs
XESCL	Product of log of real estate investment and log of industrial and commercial loans
XESPL	Product of log of real estate investment and log of personal loans
XESOT	Product of log of real estate investment and log of all other outputs

XCLPL	Product of log of industrial and commercial loans and log of personal loans
XCLOT	Product of log of industrial and commercial loans and log of all other outputs
XPLOT	Product of log of personal loans and log of all other outputs
XPACA	Product of log of average salaries and benefits and log of rental rates on capital
XPADP	Product of log of average salaries and benefits and log of interest rates on transaction accounts
XPATE	Product of log of average salaries and benefits and log of interest rates on nontransaction accounts
XPARE	Product of log of average salaries and benefits and log of the rates on the rest of the inputs
XCADP	Product of log of rental rates on capital and log of transaction accounts
XCATE	Product of log of rental rates on capital and log of interest rates on nontransaction accounts
XCARE	Product of log of rental rates on capital and log of the rates on the rest of the inputs
XDPTE	Product of log of interest rates on transaction accounts and log of interest rates on nontransaction accounts
XDPRE	Product of log of interest rates on transaction accounts and log of rates on the rest of the inputs
XESPA	Product of log of real estate investment and log of average salaries and benefits
XESCA	Product of log of real estate investment and log of rental rates on capital
XESDP	Product of log of real estate investment and log of interest rates on transaction accounts
XESTE	Product of log of real estate investment and log of interest rates on nontransaction accounts
XESRE	Product of log of real estate investment and log of rates on the rest of the inputs
XCLPA	Product of log of industrial and commercial loans and log of average salaries and benefits
XCLCA	Product of log of industrial and commercial loans and log of rental rates on capital

XCLDP	Product of log of industrial and commercial loans and log of interest rates on transaction accounts
XCLTE	Product of log of industrial and commercial loans and log of interest rates on nontransaction accounts
XCLRE	Product of log of industrial and commercial loans and log of rates on the rest of the inputs
XPLPA	Product of log of personal loan and log of average salaries and benefits
XPLCA	Product of log of personal loans and log of rental rates on capital
XPLDP	Product of log of personal loans and log of interest rates on transaction accounts
XPLTE	Product of log of personal loans and log of interest rates on nontransaction accounts
XPLRE	Product of log of personal loans and log of rates on the rest of the inputs
XOTPA	Product of log of all other outputs and log of average salaries and benefits
XOTCA	Product of log of all other outputs and log of rental rates on capital
XOTDP	Product of log of all other outputs and log of interest rates on transaction accounts
XOTTE	Product of log of all other outputs and log of interest rates on nontransaction accounts
XOTRE	Product of log of all other outputs and log of rates on the rest of the inputs
BRANCH	The number of branches

DEFINITION OF MODELS

Models	*Definitions*
LCOST	The total cost model
SWAGE	The wage share model
SCAPITAL	The capital share model
STRAN	The transaction account share model
SNONTRAN	The nontransaction account share model

Appendix D

EXAMPLES OF PERFORMANCE INDICATORS

D.1 Performance Indicators of Banking Firms

MODEL CATEGORY: NORTH/LARGE METRO/BHC/BRANCH BANKS

INDICATOR		INDICATOR	
SCALE	1.0435	SCOPE:	
MARGINAL COST	0.0448	ESTATE VS C&I	0.0438
AVERAGE COST	0.0430	ESTATE VS PRNL	-0.0574
AVERAGE INCOME	0.0500	ESTATE VS REST	0.0446
SPREAD1	0.0071	C&I VS PRNL	-0.0112
SPREAD2	0.0052	C&I VS REST	0.0235
TFP	-1.8402	PRNL VS REST	-0.0444

SCALE:Economies of scale
SCOPE:Economies of scope
SPREAD1: Spread between average income and average cost
SPREAD2: Spread between average income and marginal cost
TFP: Total factor productivity
ESTATE: Real estate loans
C&I: Commercial and industrial loans
PNRL: Personal loans
REST: Rest of banking activities

D.1   Performance Indicators of Banking Firms (Cont'd)

ELASTICITIES OF SUBSTITUTION

	LABOR	CAPITAL	TRAN	NOTRAN	OTHER
LABOR	-2.3698				
CAPITAL	1.0000	-0.3999			
TRAN	-0.5118	-0.4960	-14.8176		
NOTRAN	0.2396	-0.6491	1.3416	-0.4544	
OTHER	1.4700	1.0931	1.0000	0.8993	-4.7129

TRAN: Transaction accounts
NOTRAN: Nontransaction accounts
OTHER: All other inputs used

D.2 Performance Indicators of Banking Firms

MODEL CATEGORY: NORTH/MEDIUM METRO/BHC/BRANCH BANKS

INDICATOR		INDICATOR	
SCALE	1.1017	SCOPE:	
MARGINAL COST	0.0488	ESTATE VS C&I	0.1160
AVERAGE COST	0.0443	ESTATE VS PRNL	-0.0002
AVERAGE INCOME	0.0520	ESTATE VS REST	-0.0685
SPREAD1	0.0077	C&I VS PRNL	0.0391
SPREAD2	0.0032	C&I VS REST	-0.0302
TFP	-0.8309	PRNL VS REST	-0.0020

SCALE:Economies of scale
SCOPE:Economies of scope
SPREAD1: Spread between average income and average cost
SPREAD2: Spread between average income and marginal cost
TFP: Total factor productivity
ESTATE: Real estate loans
C&I: Commercial and industrial loans
PNRL: Personal loans
REST: Rest of banking activities

D.2   Performance Indicators of Banking Firms (Cont'd)

ELASTICITIES OF SUBSTITUTION

	LABOR	CAPITAL	TRAN	NOTRAN	OTHER
LABOR	-2.4099				
CAPITAL	0.5203	-1.0175			
TRAN	0.1334	-1.0275	-16.0044		
NOTRAN	0.2482	-0.3625	1.2437	-0.5350	
OTHER	1.4484	1.1003	1.0000	1.0000	-4.9469

TRAN: Transaction accounts
NONTRAN: Nontransaction accounts
OTHER: All other inputs used

D.3 Performance Indicators of Banking Firms

MODEL CATEGORY: NORTH/SMALL METRO/BHC/BRANCH BANKS

INDICATOR		INDICATOR	
SCALE	1.1820	SCOPE:	
MARGINAL COST	0.0527	ESTATE VS C&I	0.0228
AVERAGE COST	0.0446	ESTATE VS PRNL	-0.0236
AVERAGE INCOME	0.0509	ESTATE VS REST	-0.0265
SPREAD1	0.0062	C&I VS PRNL	-0.0096
SPREAD2	-0.0018	C&I VS REST	0.0136
TFP	-1.3052	PRNL VS REST	-0.0176

SCALE: Economies of scale
SCOPE: Economies of scope
SPREAD1: Spread between average income and average cost
SPREAD2: Spread between average income and marginal cost
TFP: Total factor productivity
ESTATE: Real estate loans
C&I: Commercial and industrial loans
PNRL: Personal loans
REST: Rest of banking activities

D.3   Performance Indicators of Banking Firms (Cont'd)

ELASTICITIES OF SUBSTITUTION

	LABOR	CAPITAL	TRAN	NOTRAN	OTHER
LABOR	-2.9384				
CAPITAL	0.3196	0.3244			
TRAN	-0.7181	-0.8040	-10.9672		
NOTRAN	0.5947	-0.4078	1.3233	-0.6742	
OTHER	1.3564	1.1015	1.3453	1.0000	-4.9357

TRAN: Transaction accounts
NOTRAN: Nontransaction accounts
OTHER: All other inputs used

D.4   Performance Indicators of Banking Firms

MODEL CATEGORY: NORTH/LARGE METRO/BHC/UNIT BANKS

INDICATOR		INDICATOR	
SCALE	0.8937	SCOPE:	
MARGINAL COST	0.0373	ESTATE VS C&I	0.0271
AVERAGE COST	0.0417	ESTATE VS PRNL	0.0694
AVERAGE INCOME	0.0493	ESTATE VS REST	-0.1329
SPREAD1	0.0075	C&I VS PRNL	0.0806
SPREAD2	0.0120	C&I VS REST	-0.0401
TFP	0.4965	PRNL VS REST	-0.0569

SCALE: Economies of scale
SCOPE: Economies of scope
SPREAD1: Spread between average income and average cost
SPREAD2: Spread between average income and marginal cost
TFP: Total factor productivity
ESTATE: Real estate loans
C&I: Commercial and industrial loans
PNRL: Personal loans
REST: Rest of banking activities

D.4   Performance Indicators of Banking Firms (Cont'd)

ELASTICITIES OF SUBSTITUTION

	LABOR	CAPITAL	TRAN	NOTRAN	OTHER
LABOR	-2.3034				
CAPITAL	1.0000	-3.3936			
TRAN	0.0596	-0.9668	-14.2255		
NOTRAN	0.2611	-0.1912	1.3016	-0.4116	
OTHER	1.4628	0.8653	1.0000	0.6182	-4.2732

TRAN: Transaction accounts
NOTRAN: Nontransaction accounts
OTHER: All other inputs used

D.5 Performance Indicators of Banking Firms

MODEL CATEGORY: NORTH/MEDIUM METRO/BHC/UNIT BANKS

INDICATORS		INDICATOR	
SCALE	1.2768	SCOPE:	
MARGINAL COST	0.0524	ESTATE VS C&I	-0.0327
AVERAGE COST	0.0411	ESTATE VS PRNL	0.0654
AVERAGE INCOME	0.0489	ESTATE VS REST	-0.1333
SPREAD1	0.0078	C&I VS PRNL	-0.0231
SPREAD2	-0.0035	C&I VS REST	0.0000
TFP	3.7279	PRNL VS REST	-0.0323

SCALE: Economies of scale
SCOPE: Economies of scope
SPREAD1: Spread between average income and average cost
SPREAD2: Spread between average income and marginal cost
TFP: Total factor productivity
ESTATE: Real estate loans
C&I: Commercial and industrial loans
PNRL: Personal loans
REST: Rest of banking activities

D.5   Performance Indicators of Banking Firms (Cont'd)

ELASTICITIES OF SUBSTITUTION

	LABOR	CAPITAL	TRAN	NOTRAN	OTHER
LABOR	-2.2684				
CAPITAL	0.5512	-1.5669			
TRAN	-0.6186	0.6187	-8.9388		
NOTRAN	0.4609	-0.3548	1.6144	-0.6394	
OTHER	1.0000	0.8401	-1.3307	1.0000	-5.2746

TRAN: Transaction accounts
NOTRAN: Nontransaction accounts
OTHER: All other inputs used

D.6   Performance Indicators of Banking Firms

MODEL CATEGORY: NORTH/SMALL METRO/BHC/UNIT BANKS

INDICATORS		INDICATOR	
SCALE	0.9909	SCOPE:	
MARGINAL COST	0.0456	ESTATE VS C&I	0.0939
AVERAGE COST	0.0460	ESTATE VS PRNL	0.0215
AVERAGE INCOME	0.0480	ESTATE VS REST	-0.1152
SPREAD1	0.0020	C&I VS PRNL	0.0341
SPREAD2	0.0024	C&I VS REST	-0.0688
TFP	9.0874	PRNL VS REST	-0.0732

SCALE: Economies of scale
SCOPE: Economies of scope
SPREAD1: Spread between average income and average cost
SPREAD2: Spread between average income and marginal cost
TFP: Total factor productivity
ESTATE: Real estate loans
C&I: Commercial and industrial loans
PNRL: Personal loans
REST: Rest of banking activities

D.6   Performance Indicators of Banking Firms (Cont'd)

ELASTICITIES OF SUBSTITUTION

	LABOR	CAPITAL	TRAN	NOTRAN	OTHER
LABOR	-3.2724				
CAPITAL	1.0000	-2.7527			
TRAN	-0.9711	-0.5615	-10.4245		
NOTRAN	1.0000	-0.2731	1.4278	-0.6173	
OTHER	1.3165	1.0000	1.0000	0.7545	-4.9845

TRAN: Transction accounts
NOTRAN: Nontransaction accounts
OTHER: All other inputs used

D.7 Performance Indicators of Banking Firms

MODEL CATEGORY: NORTH/LARGE METRO/NONBHC/BRANCH
BANKS

INDICATOR		INDICATOR	
SCALE	0.9237	SCOPE:	
MARGINAL COST	0.0392	ESTATE VS C&I	0.0214
AVERAGE COST	0.0425	ESTATE VS PRNL	0.0361
AVERAGE INCOME	0.0455	ESTATE VS REST	-0.0017
SPREAD1	0.0030	C&I VS PRNL	0.0120
SPREAD2	0.0063	C&I VS REST	0.0262
TFP	-3.1800	PRNL VS REST	0.0150

SCALE: Economies of scale
SCOPE: Economies of scope
SPREAD1: Spread between average income and average cost
SPREAD2: Spread between average income and marginal cost
TFP: Total factor productivity
ESTATE: Real estate loans
C&I: Commercial and industrial loans
PNRL: Personal loans
REST: Rest of banking activities

D.7   Performance Indicators of Banking Firms (Cont'd)

ELASTICITIES OF SUBSTITUTION

	LABOR	CAPITAL	TRAN	NOTRAN	OTHER
LABOR	-1.9779				
CAPITAL	1.0000	-0.5278			
TRAN	-0.6779	-1.0329	-18.8100		
NOTRAN	0.1030	-0.5728	1.3009	-0.3429	
OTHER	1.3321	1.0000	1.0000	1.0000	-5.7262

TRAN: Transaction accounts
NOTRAN: Nontransaction accounts
OTHER: All other inputs used

D.8 Performance Indicators of Banking Firms

MODEL CATEGORY: NORTH/MEDIUM/NONBHC/BRANCH BANKS

INDICATOR		INDICATOR	
SCALE	2.2238	SCOPE:	
MARGINAL COST	0.0956	ESTATE VS C&I	0.0000
AVERAGE COST	0.0430	ESTATE VS PRNL	0.0000
AVERAGE INCOME	0.0478	ESTATE VS REST	-0.1762
SPREAD1	0.0048	C&I VS PRNL	0.0000
SPREAD2	-0.0478	C&I VS REST	0.2450
TFP	-1.2398	PRNL VS REST	-0.0836

SCALE: Economies of scale
SCOPE: Economies of scope
SPREAD1: Spread between average income and average cost
SPREAD2: Spread between average income and marginal cost
TFP: Total factor productivity
ESTATE: Real estate loans
C&I: Commercial and industrial loans
PNRL: Personal loans
REST: Rest of banking activities

D.8   Performance Indicators of Banking Firms (Cont'd)

ELASTICITIES OF SUBSTITUTION

	LABOR	CAPITAL	TRAN	NOTRAN	OTHER
LABOR	-1.3959				
CAPITAL	1.0000	-0.9516			
TRAN	-0.3364	1.0000	-17.2070		
NOTRAN	-0.2174	-0.4086	1.2031	-0.3920	
OTHER	1.5605	1.0000	1.0000	1.0000	-5.9449

TRAN: Transaction accounts
NOTRAN: Nontransaction accounts
OTHER: All other inputs used

D.9   Performance Indicators of Banking Firms

MODEL CATEGORY: NORTH/LARGE METRO/NONBHC/UNIT
BANKS

INDICATOR		INDICATOR	
SCALE	0.9719	SCOPE:	
MARGINAL COST	0.0423	ESTATE VS C&I	0.1487
AVERAGE COST	0.0435	ESTATE VS PRNL	-0.0203
AVERAGE INCOME	0.0464	ESTATE VS REST	-0.4327
SPREAD1	0.0029	C&I VS PRNL	0.0000
SPREAD2	0.0041	C&I VS REST	-0.1002
TFP	2.2031	PRNL VS REST	0.0215

SCALE: Economies of scale
SCOPE: Economies of scope
SPREAD1: Spread between average income and average cost
SPREAD2: Spread between average income and marginal cost
TFP: Total factor productivity
ESTATE: Real estate loans
C&I: Commercial and industrial loans
PNRL: Personal loans
REST: Rest of banking activities

D.9   Performance Indicators of Banking Firms (Cont'd)

ELASTICITIES OF SUBSTITUTION

	LABOR	CAPITAL	TRAN	NOTRAN	OTHER
LABOR	-2.0073				
CAPITAL	-2.4410	-4.8166			
TRAN	-0.9853	-2.3972	-14.7722		
NOTRAN	0.3588	0.6323	1.5447	-0.5257	
OTHER	1.5855	0.7896	1.0000	0.6244	-4.5804

TRAN: Transaction accounts
NOTRAN: Nontransaction accounts
OTHER: All other inputs used

D.10   Performance Indicators of Banking Firms

MODEL CATEGORY: NORTH/MEDIUM METRO/NONBHC/UNIT
BANKS

INDICATOR		INDICATOR	
SCALE	0.9878	SCOPE:	
MARGINAL COST	0.0424	ESTATE VS C&I	0.0916
AVERAGE COST	0.0430	ESTATE VS PRNL	0.0945
AVERAGE INCOME	0.0478	ESTATE VS REST	-0.1810
SPREAD1	0.0048	C&I VS PRNL	0.0389
SPREAD2	0.0054	C&I VS REST	0.1043
TFP	-0.5107	PRNL VS REST	0.0802

SCALE: Economies of scale
SCOPE: Economies of scope
SPREAD1: Spread between average income and average cost
SPREAD2: Spread between average income and marginal cost
TFP: Total factor productivity
ESTATE: Real estate loans
C&I: Commercial and industrial loans
PNRL: Personal loans
REST: Rest of banking activities

D.10   Performance Indicators of Banking Firms (Cont'd)

ELASTICITIES OF SUBSTITUTION

	LABOR	CAPITAL	TRAN	NOTRAN	OTHER
LABOR	-2.5220				
CAPITAL	1.0000	-2.8654			
TRAN	-0.3682	-1.2110	-15.6056		
NOTRAN	0.3182	-0.1939	1.3391	-0.3992	
OTHER	1.3784	0.6176	1.0000	0.7537	-4.7419

TRAN: Transaction accounts
NOTRAN: Nontransaction accounts
OTHER: All other inputs used

D.11   Performance Indicators of Banking Firms

MODEL CATEGORY: NORTH/SMALL METRO/NONBHC/UNIT
BANKS

INDICATOR		INDICATOR	
SCALE	1.0010	SCOPE:	
MARGINAL COST	0.0424	ESTATE VS C&I	-0.1512
AVERAGE COST	0.0424	ESTATE VS PRNL	-0.2709
AVERAGE INCOME	0.0474	ESTATE VS REST	1.4095
SPREAD1	0.0051	C&I VS PRNL	0.0768
SPREAD2	0.0050	C&I VS REST	-0.3924
TFP	-8.3392	PRNL VS REST	-0.5600

SCALE: Economies of scale
SCOPE: Economies of scope
SPREAD1: Spread between average income and average cost
SPREAD2: Spread between average income and marginal cost
TFP: Total factor productivity
ESTATE: Real estate loans
C&I: Commercial and industrial loans
PNRL: Personal loans
REST: Rest of banking activities

D.11 Performance Indicators of Banking Firms (Cont'd)

ELASTICITIES OF SUBSTITUTION

	LABOR	CAPITAL	TRAN	NOTRAN	OTHER
LABOR	-2.7310				
CAPITAL	1.7174	-6.5337			
TRAN	-0.1283	-2.7920	-13.6696		
NOTRAN	0.2964	0.1416	1.2381	-0.3678	
OTHER	1.8247	0.5641	1.7354	0.6192	-6.1146

TRAN: Transaction accounts
NOTRAN: Nontransaction accounts
OTHER: All other inputs used

References

Adar, Z., Agmon, T., and Orgler, Y.E. 1975. "Output Mix and Jointness in Production in the Banking Firm." *Journal of Money, Credit, and Banking* 7: 235-243.

Aivazian, V.A., Callen, J.L., Chan, M.W.L., and Mountain, D.C. 1987. "Economies of Scale Versus Technological Change in the Natural Gas Transmission Industry." *Review of Economics and Statistics* 69: 556-561.

Alonso, W. 1964. *Location and Land Use*. Cambridge: Harvard University Press.

Anderson, S.P., de Palma, A. and Thisse, J.F. 1989. "Demand for Differentiated Products, Discrete Choice Models, and the Characteristics Approach." *Review of Economic Studies* 56: 21-35.

Anderson, S.P. 1985. "Product Choice With Economies of Scope." *Regional Science and Urban Economics* 15: 277-294.

--. 1987. "Spatial Competition and Price Leadership." *International Journal of Industrial Organization* 5: 369-398.

Archilbald, G.C., Eaton, B.C., and Lipsey, R.G. 1986. Address Models of Value Theory. In *New Developments in the Analysis of Market Structure*. E.E. Stiglitz and G.F. Mathenwson Ed. Cambridge: MIT Press.

Arrow, K. J., Chenery, H. B., Minhas, B., and Solow, R.M. 1961. "Capital-Labor Substitution and Economic Efficiency." *Review of Economics and Statistics* 43: 225-250.

Arrow, K.J. and Debreu, G. 1954. "Existence of An Equilibrium for A Competitive Economy." *Econometrica* 22: 265-290.

Arrow, K.J. and Intriligator, M.D. 1982. *Handbook of Mathematical Economics*. New York: North-Holland Publishing Co.

Bailey, E.E. and Friedlaener, F. 1982. "Market Structure and Multiproduct Industries." *Journal of Economic Literature* 20: 1024-1028.

Baltensperger, E. 1972. "Economies of Scale, Firm Size, and Concentration in Banking." *Journal of Money, Credit, and Banking* 4: 467-488.

Baumol, W.J., Panzar, J.C., and Willig, R.D. 1982. *Contestable Markets and the Theory of Industry Structure.* New York: Harcourt Brace Jovanovich, Inc.

Beattie, Bruce R. and Taylor, C. Robert. 1985. *Economics of Production.* New York: John Wiley & Sons, Inc.

Beckmann, M.J., 1976. Spatial Equilibrium in the Dispersed City. In *Mathematical Land Use Theory.* G.J. Papageorgiou Ed. Lexington: Lezington Books.

Bell, F.W. and Murphy, N.B., 1968. *Costs in Commercial Banking: A Quantitative Analysis of Bank Behavior and its Relation to Bank Regulation.* Research Report No. 41. Boston: Federal Reserve Bank of Boston.

Benston, G.J. 1985. "The Cost of Banking Oprerations and Interstate Banking." In *Commercial Banking and Interstate Expansion.* Frieder, L.A. *et al.* Ed. Ann Arbor, MI: UMI Research Press.

Benston, G.J., Hanweck, G.A., and Humphrey, D.B. 1982. "Scale Economies in Banking." *Journal of Money, Credit, and Banking* 14: 435-456.

Benston, G.J. 1972. "Economies of Scale of Financial Institutions." *Journal of Money, Credit, and Banking* 4: 312-341.

Berger, Allen N. and Humphrey, David B. 1991. "The Dominance of Inefficiencies Over Scale and Product Mix Economies in Banking." *Journal of Monetary Economics* 28: 117-148.

Berndt, E.R., and Christensen, L.R. 1973. "The Translog Function and the Substitution of Equipment, Structures, and Labor in U.S. Manufacturing 1929-68." *Journal of Econometrics* 1: 81-114.

Berry, B. and Pred, A. 1961. *Central Place Studies.* Philadelphia: Regional Science Institute.

Black, R.P. 1991. "Reflections of Deposit Insurance." *Economic Review* 77: 3-6. Richmond: Federal Reserve Bank of Richmond.

Blair, R.D. and Kaserman, D.L. 1985. *Antitrust Economics.* Homewood, IL: Richard D. Irwin, Inc.

Bonbright, J.C. and Means. G.C. 1969. *The Holding Company.* New York: Augustus M. Kelley Publishers.

Borchert, J.R.. 1972. "America's Changing Metropolitan Regions." *Annals, Association of American Geographers* 62: 352-373.

--. 1978. "Major Control Points in American Economic Geography. *Annals, Association of American Geographers* 68: 22-32.

Bosworth, Derek L. 1976. *Production Functions*. Westmead, England: Saxon House.

Boyd, J.H. and Graham, S.L. 1991. "Investigating the Banking Consolidation Trend." *Quarterly Review* Spring: 3-15. Minneapolis: Federal Reserve Bank of Minneapolis.

Brander, J.A. and Eaton, J. 1984. "Product Line Rivalry." *American Economic Review* 74: 323-324.

Buono, M.J. and Eakin, B.K. 1990. "Branching Restrictions and Banking Costs." *Journal of Banking and Finance* 14: 1151-1162.

Carlino, G.A., 1978. *Economies of Scale in Manufacturing Location*. Boston: Kluwer Boston Inc.

Cartinhour, Gaines T. and Westerfield, Ray B. 1980. *Branch, Group and Chain Banking and Historical Survey of Branch Banking in the United States*. New York: Aron Press.

Caves, D.W., Christensen, L.R., and Diewert, W.E. 1982. "The Economic Theory of Index number and the Measurement of Input, Output, and Productivity." *Econometrics* 50: 1393-1414.

Caves, D.W., and Christensen, L.R. 1980. "Global Properties of Flexible Functional Forms." *American Economic Review* 70: 422-432.

CDA Investment Technologies Inc. 1992. *Mutual Funds Panorama*. Rockville, MD: CDA Investment Technologies Inc.

--. 1992. *Spectrum Directory of Investment*. Rockville, MD: CDA Investment Technologies Inc.

Chamberlin, E.H., 1932, *The Theory of Monopolistic Competition*. Cambridge: Harvard University Press.

Christaller, W., 1966. *Central Places in Southern Germany*. Englwood Cliffs: Prentice-Hall.

Christensen, L.R., Jorgensen, D.W., and Lau, L.J. 1973. "Transcendental Logarithmic Production Frontiers." *The Review of Economics and Statistics* 55: 28-45.

Clarke, I.M. 1985. *The Spatial Organization of Multinational Corporations*. New York: St. Martin's Press.

Clark, J.A. 1984. "Estimation of Economies of Scale in Banking Using A Generalized Functional Form." *Journal of Money, Credit, and Banking* 16: 51-67.

Coase, R., 1937. "The Nature of the Firm." *Economica* 4: 386-405.

Compton, E.N. 1987. *The New World of Commercial Banking.* Lexington, MA: D.C. Heath and Company.

Corrigan, E.G. 1992. "The Legacy of the 1980s." *Quarterly Review* 17: 1-4. New York: Federal Reserve Bank of New York.

Cornes, R., and Sandler, T. 1986. *The Theory of Externalities, Public Goods, and Club Goods.* Cambridge: University Press.

Crawford, R.D. and Sihler, W.W. 1991. *The Troubled Money Business.* New York: HaperCollins Publishers

Debreu, G. 1959. *Theory of Value.* New York: Wiley.

Denny, M. and Fuss, M. 1983. "A General Approach to Intertemporal and Interspatial Productivity Comparisons." *Journal of Econometrics* 23: 315-330.

Department of the Treasury, 1981. *Geographic Restrictions on Commercial Banking in the United States.* Washington D.C.: Department of the Treasure.

Diewert, W.E. 1976. "Exact and Superlative Index Numbers." *Journal of Econometrics* 4: 115-145.

--. 1971. "An Application of the Shephard Duality Theorem: a Generalized Leontief Production Function." *Journal of Political Economy* 79: 481-507.

Doll, John P. and Orazem, Frank. 1984. *Production Economics* 2nd Ed. New York: John Wiley & Sons.

Douglas, J.A. and Binder-Arain, L. 1993. *Federal Banking Laws.* Boston: Warren Gorham Lamont.

Eccles, R.G., and Crane, D.B. 1988. *Doing Deals.* Boston: Harvard Business School Press.

Edwards, F.R. 1986. Concentration in Banking: Problem With Solution? In *Deregulating Financial Services.* G.G Kaufman and R.C. Kormand Ed. Cambridg: Ballinger Publishing Co.

Eisenbeis, R.A. 1985. An Analysis of Regional Approaches to Interstate Banking. In *Commercial Banking and Interstate Expansion.* Frieder, L.A. *et al.* Ed. Ann Arbor, MI: UMI Research Press.

Emerson, D.L. 1973. "Optimum Firm Location and the Theory of Production." *Journal of Regional Science* 13: 335-347.

Federal Reserve Bank of Atlanta. 1985. *Interstate Banking.* Westpoint, Conn.: Quorum Books.

Fischer, G.C. 1961. *Bank Holding Companies.* New York: Columbia University Press.

Fisher, I. 1922. *The Making of Index Numbers.* Boston: Houghton-Mifflin.

Fraser, D.R. and Kolari, J.W. 1985. *The Future of Small Banks in A Deregulated Environment.* Cambridg: Ballinger Publishing Co.

Frieder, L.A. *et al.* 1985. *Commercial Banking and Interstate Expansion.* Ann Arbor, MI: UMI Press.

Frieder, L.A., Apilado, V.P. 1982. "Bank Holding Company Research: Classification, Synthesis and New Directions." *Journal of Bank Research* summer: 80-95.

Friedman, D.H. 1991. *A Preface to Banking.* Washington DC: American Banker Association.

Fujita, M., 1990. Spatial Interactions and Agglomeration in Urban Economies. In *New Frontiers in Regional Science* M. Chatterji and R.E. Kuenne Ed. New York: New York University Press.

--. 1988. "A Monopolistic Competitive Model of Agglomeration: Differentiated Product Approach." *Regional Science and Urban Economics* 18: 87-124.

Fujita, M and Thisse, J.F., 1991. "Spatial Duopoly and Residential Structure." *Journal of Urban Economics* 30: 27-47.

Fujita, M. 1984. Urban Land Use Theory. In *Location Theory.* J.J. Gabszeiwice *et al.* Ed. New York: Hardwood Publishing Co.

Fujita, M. 1981. Location of Firms With Input Transactions." *Environment and Planning A* 18: 1401-1414.

Garten, H.A. 1991. *Why Bank Regulation Failed.* New York: Quorrum Books.

Gilligan, Thomas W. 1984. "An Empirical Study of Joint Production and Scale Economies in Commercial Banking." *Journal of Banking and Finance* 8: 67-77.

Gilligan, T.W. and Smirlock, M.L. 1984. "An Empirical Study of Joint Production and Scale Economies in Commercial Banking." *Journal of Banking and Finance* 8: 67-77.

Glaister, S. 1984. *Mathematical Methods for Economists* 3rd Ed. New York: Basil Blackwell.

Golembe, C.H. 1992. *The Golembe Reports.* Delray Beach, FL: CHG Consulting Inc.

Golembe, C.H. and Holland, D.S. 1986. *Federal Regulation of Banking: 1986-87.* Washington D.C.: Golembe Associates, Inc.

Goldman, S. M. Uzawa, H. 1964. "A Note on Separability in Demand Analysis." *Econometrica* 32: 387-398.

Gourgues, Jr. H.W. and Lauterbach, J.R. 1987. *Revolution in Financial Services.* Washington D.C.: The Bureau of National Affairs.

Graddy, D.B. and Spencer, A.H. 1990. *Managing Commercial Banks.* Englewood Cliffs, New Jersey: Prentice Hall.

Graddy, D.B. 1979. *The Bank Holding Company Performance Controversy.* Washington DC: University Press of America, Inc.

Greenbaum, S.I. 1967. "A Study of Bank Cost." *National Banking Review* 4: 415-434.

Greene, W.H. 1993. *Econometric Analysis.* New York: Macmillan Publishing Co.

Greenhut, M.L., and Ohta, H. 1975. *Theory of Spatial Pricing and Market Areas.* Durham: Duke University Press.

Greenhut, M.L., Norman, G., and Hung, Chao-shun. 1987. *The Economics of Imperfect Competition: A Spatial Approach.* Cambridge: Cambridge University Press.

Gropper, D.M. 1991. "An Empirical Investigation of Changes in Scale Economies for the Commercial Banking Firm, 1979-1986." *Journal of Money, Credit, and Banking* 23: 718-727.

Gruson, M. and Reisner, R. 1991. *Regulation of Foreign Banks.* Salem, New Hampshire: Butterworth Legal Publishers.

Haining, R.P. 1983. "Modeling Intra-urban Price Competition: An Example of Gasoline Retailing." *Journal of Regional Science* 23: 271-292.

Hamill, P.J. and Pollock, E.R. 1991. *Banking Law Journal Digest.* New York: Warren, Gorham & Lamont.

Hayes, S.L., and Hubbard, P.M. 1990. *Investment Banking.* Boston: Harvard Business School Press.

Hawawini, G., and Swary, I. 1990. *Mergers and Acquisitions in the U.S. Banking Industry.* New York: North-Holland.

Haywood, C.F. 1973. Structural and Competitive Objectives. In *The Bank Holding Company.* R.B. Johnson Ed. Dallas: SMU Press.

Hetzel, R.L. 1991. "Too Big to Fail: Origins, Consequences, and Outlook." *Economic Review* 77: 3-13. Richmond: Federal Reserve Bank of Richmond.

Holly, B.P. 1987. "Regulation, Competition, and Technology: the Restructuring of the US Commercial Banking System." *Environment and Planning A* 19: 633-652.

Hove, A.C., Jr. 1994. Testimony Before the Committee on Banking, Housing, and Urban Affairs, U.S. Senate. In *Interstate Banking and Insurance Activities of National Banks*. Washington DC: U.S. Government Printing Offices.

Humphery, D.B. 1991. "Productivity in Banking and Efforts From Deregulation" *Economic Review* 77. Richmond: Federal Reserve Bank of Richmond.

--. 1984. *The U.S. Payments System: Costs, Pricing, Competition and Risk*. New York: New York University.

Hunter, W.C. and Timme, S.G. 1986. "Technical Change, Organizational Form, and the Structure of Bank Production." *Journal of Money, Credit, and Banking* 18: 152-166.

Investment Company Institute. 1990. *Guide to Mutual Funds*. Washington, D.C.

Isard, W. 1956. *Location and Space Economy*. New York: MIT Press and John wiley and Sons.

Jessee, M.A. and Seelig, S.A. 1977. *Bank Holding Companies and the Public Interest*. Lexington, MA: Lexington Books.

Jorgenson, D.W., and Nishimizu, M. 1978. "U.S. and Japanese Economic Growth, 1952-1974: An International Comparison." *The Economic Journal* 88: 707-726.

Kamerschen, David R., 1992. *Money and Banking* 10th Ed. Cincinnati: South-Western Publishing Co.

Kaufman, G.G. 1993. Diminishing Role of Commercial Banking in the U.S. Economy, In *The Crisis in American Banking*. L.H. White Ed. New York: New York University Press.

--. 1983. *The U.S. Financial System* 2nd Ed. Englewood Cliffs, NJ: Prentice-Hall, Inc.

Kindleberger, C.P. 1983. "International Banks as Leaders or Followers of International Business." *Journal of Banking and Finance* 7: 583-596.

King, B.F., Tschinkel, S.L., and Whitehead, D.D. 1989. "Interstate Banking Development." *Economic Review* May/June: 32-44. Atlanta: Federal Reserve Bank of Atlanta.

Klebanner, B.J. 1990. *American Commercial Banking: A History*. Boston: Twayne Publishers.

Kogiku, K.C. 1982. *Microeconomic Models*. Malabar, FL: Robert E. Krieger Publishing Co.

Kohn, M. 1991. *Money, Banking, and Financial Markets*. Hinsdal, IL: The Dryden Press.

Kolari, J. and Zardkoohi, A. 1987. *Bank Costs, Structure, and Performance*. Lexington, MA: Lexington Books.

Kolari, J., McInish, T.H., and Saniga, E.M. 1989. "A Note on the Distribution Types of Financial Ratios in the Commercial Banking Industry." *Journal of Banking and Finance* 13, 463-471.

Krmenec A.J. and Esparza A. 1993. "Modeling Interaction in a System of Markets." *Geographical Analysis* 25: 354-368.

Laderman, E.S., and Pozdena, R.J. 1991. "Interstate Banking and Competition." *Economic Review* Spring: 32-47. San Francisco: Federal Reserve Bank of San Francisco.

Laderman, E.S., Schmidt, R.H., and Zimmerman, G.C. 1991. "Location, Branching, and Bank Portfolio Diversification: the Case of Agricultural Lending." *Economic Review* Winter: 24-37. San Francisco: Federal Reserve Bank of San Francisco.

LaWare, J.P. 1994. Testimony Before the Committee on Banking, Housing, and Urban Affairs, U.S. Senate. In *Interstate Banking and Insurance Activities of National Banks*. Washington DC: U.S. Government Printing Offices.

Lekachman, Robert, 1959. *A History of Economic Ideas*. New York: Harper & Brothers, Publishers.

Leontief, W.W. 1947. "Introduction to A Theory of the Internal Structure of Functional Relationships." *Econometrica* 15: 361-373.

Li, Yuanchuan. 1987. *Principles of Microeconomics*. Beijing: Beijing University Press.

Litan, R.E. 1987. *What Should Banks Do?* Washington DC: the Brookings Institution.

Longbrake, W.A. and Haslem, J.A. 1975. "Productive Efficiency in Commercial Banking: The Effects of Size and Legal Form of Organization on the Cost of Producing Demand Deposit Services." *Journal of Money, Credit, and Banking* 7: 317-330.

Lord, J.D. 1990. "Impact of Banking Acquisitions on Local Market Concentration in Florida." *Southeastern Geographer* 30: 1-16.

--. 1992. "Geographic Deregulation of the U.S. Banking Industry and Spatial Transfers of Corporate Control." *Urban Geography* 13: 25-48.

Lösch, A., 1954, *The Economics of Location*. New Haven: Yale University Press.

Lovell, C.A.K. and Sickles, R.C. 1983. "Testing Efficiency Hypothesis in Joint Production: a Joint Parametric Approach." *The Review of Economics and Statistics* 65: 51-58.

Lowry, I.S. 1964. *A Model of Metropolis RM-4035-RC*. Santa Monica, CA: Rand Corporation.

Ludwig, E.A. 1994. Testimony Before the Committee on Banking, Housing, and Urban Affairs, U.S. Senate. In *Interstate Banking and Insurance Activities of National Banks*. Washington DC: U.S. Government Printing Offices.

Lundsten, Lorman L. 1978. *Market Share Forecasting for Banking Office*. UMI Research Press.

Mai, Chao-Cheng, 1981. "Optimal Location and the Theory of the Firm Under Demand Uncertainty." *Regional Science and Urban Economics* 11: 549-557.

Marimont, Martin L. 1969. Measuring Real Output for Industrial Providing Services: OBE Concepts and Methods. In *Production and Productivity in the Service Industries*. Victor R. Fuchs Ed. New York: National Bureau of Economic Research.

Marshall, A., 1920, *Principles of Economics* 8th Ed. London: Macmillan & Co.

Martz, D.J.F., and Semple, R. K., 1985, "Hierarchical Corporate Decision-making Structure Within the Canadian Urban System: the Case of Banking." *Urban Geography* 6: 316-330.

Mengle, D.L. 1990. "The Case for Interstate Branch Banking." *Economic Review* 76 (6): 3-16. Richmond: Federal Reserve Bank of Richmond.

--. 1989. "Banking Under Changing Rules: the Fifth Districts Since 1970." *Economic Review* 75(2): 3-7. Richmond: Federal Reserve Bank of Richmond.

Miller, R.B. 1990a. *The Prentice Hall Banking Yearbook*. Englewood Cliffs, New Jersey: Prentice-Hall.

--. 1990b. *American Banking in Crisis*. Homewood, IL: Dow Jones-Irwin.

Mintz, B., and Schwartz, M., 1983. "Financial Interest Groups and Interlocking Directorates." *Social Science History* 7: 182-204.

Mizruchi, M.S., 1982. *The American Corporate Network, 1904-1974*. Beverly Hills, CA: Sage Publications.

Moomaw, R.L., 1985, "Firm Location and City Size: Reduced Productivity Advantages as a Factor in the Decline of Manufacturing in Urban Areas." *Journal of Urban Economics* 17: 73-89.

--. 1986. "Have Changes in Localization Economics Been Responsible for Declining Productivity Advantages in Large Cities?" *Journal of Regional Science* 26: 19-23.

Miller, R.B. 1990. *The Prentice Hall Banking Yearbook*. Englewood Cliffs, NJ: Prentice Hall.

Morrison, C. 1993. *A Microeconomic Approach to the Measurement of Economic Performance*. New York: Springer-Veriag.

Moses, L., 1958, "Location and the Theory of Production." *Quarterly Journal of Economics* 72: 1180-1188.

Murphy, J.D. and White, R.W. 1983. "Economies of Scale and Economies of Scope in Multiproduct Financial Institutions: A Study of British Columbia Credit Unions." *Journal of Finance* 38: 887-902.

Murphy, N.B. 1972. "Cost of Banking Activities: Interactions Between Risks and Operating Costs, A Comment." *Journal of Money, Credit, and Banking* Aug.: 614-615.

Mussa, M. 1986. Competition, Efficiency, and Fairness in the financial Service Industry. In *Deregulating Financial Services* G.G Kaufman and R.C. Kormand Ed. Cambridge: Ballinger Publishing Co.

Muth, R. 1961. "The Spatial Structure of the Housing Market." *Papers and Proceedings of the Regional Science Association* 7:

Nelson, R.W. 1985. Branching, Scale Economies, and Banking Costs. *Journal of Banking and Finance* 9: 177-191.

Nystuen, J.D. and Dacey, M.F. 1961. "A Graph Theory Interpretation of Model Regions." *Papers of the Regional Science Association* 7: 29-42.

Ohlin, B. 1933. *Interregional and International Trade*. Cambridge: Harvard University Press.

Osborne, D. K. 1988. "Competition and Geographic Integration in Commercial Bank Lending." *Journal of Banking and Finance* 12: 85-103.

Panzar, J.C. and Willig, R.D. 1977. "Economies of Scale in Multi-output Production." *Quarterly Journal of Economics* 91: 481-493.

Park, K, and Mathur, V. 1988. "Production Technology Uncertainty and the Optimal Location of the Firm, *Journal of Regional Science* 28: 51-64.

Park, S. 1992. *Contagion of Bank Failures*. New York: Garland Publishing Co.

Park, Y.S. and Zwick, J. 1985. *International Banking in Theory and Practice*. Reading, MA: Addison-Wesley Pub. Co.

Pierce, J.L. 1991a. *The Future of Banking*. New Haven, MA: Yale University Press.

--. 1991b. Can Banks be Insulated From Nonbank Affiliates? In *Governing Bank's Future: Market vs. Regulation*. C. England Ed. Boston: Kluwer Academic Publishers.

Rhoades, S.A. 1985. "Mergers and Acquisitions by Commercial Banks, 1960-1983. *Staff Study* 142. Washington, D.C.: Federal Reserve Board.

--. 1982. "Bank Expansion and Merger Activity by State, 1960-1975." *Journal of Bank Research* 12: 254-256.

Ricardo, D., 1911, *Principles of Political Economy and Taxation*. London: J. M. Dent & Sons.

Richardson, H.W. 1979. *Regional Economics*. Urbana, IL: University of Illinois Press.

Robinson, J. 1933, *The Economics of Imperfect Competition*. London: Collier-Macmillan.

Rogers, D. 1993. T*he Future of American Banking*. New York: McGraw-Hill Inc.

Rose, Peter S. 1989. *The Interstate Banking Revolution*. New York: Quorum Books.

Ross, C. 1992. *The Urban System and Networks of Corporate Control*. Greenwich, CT: Jai Press Inc.

Saer, H. and Gregorash, S.F. 1986. *Toward Nationwide Banking*. Chicago: Federal Reserve Bank of Chicago.

Sakashita, N. 1987, Optimum Location of Public Facilities Under the Influence of the Land Market. *Journal of Regional Science* 27: 1-12.

Samuelson, P. 1952. "Spatial Price Equilibrium and Linear Programming." *American Economic Review* 42: 283-303.

Sato, R. and Nono, T. 1983. *Invariance Principles and the Structure of Technology*. New York: Springer-Verlag.

Saunders, A. and Walter, I. 1994. *Universal Banking in the United States*. New York: Oxford University Press.

Sawers, L. and Tabb, W. K., 1984, *Sunbelt/Snowbelt: Urban Development and Regional Restructuring*. New York: Oxford University Press.

Schmalensee, R. and Willig, R.D. 1989. *Handbook of Industrial Organization* 1. Netherlands: Elsevier Science Publishers B.V.

Schweizer, U., Varaiya, P., and Hartwick, J. 1976. "General Equilibrium and Location Theory." *Journal of Urban Economics*. 3: 285-303.

Scott, A. 1988. "Flexible Production Systems and Regional Development: the Rise of New Industrial Space in North America and Western Europe." *International Journal of Urban and Regional Research* 12: 173-185.

Sealey, C.W., Jr. and Lindley, James T. 1977. "Inputs, Outputs, and a Theory of Production and Cost at Depository Financial Institutions." *Journal of Finance* 32: 1251-1266.

Segal, D. 1976. "Are There Returns to Scale in City Size?" *Review of Economics and Statistics* 58: 339-350.

Sellers, B.L. 1988. *Banking: the Challenges of the Future*. New York: Vantage Press.

Semple, R.K. and Phipps, A.G. 1982. "The Spatial Evolution of Corporate Headquarters Within An Urban System." *Urban Geography* 3: 258-279.

Shefer, D. 1973. "Localization Economies in SMSAs: A Production Function Analysis." *Journal of Regional Science* 13: 55-64.

Sheppard, E. and Haining, R.P. and Plummer, P. 1992. "Spatial Pricing in Interdependent Markets." *Journal of Regional Science* 32: 55-75.

Shephard, R.W. 1953. *Cost and Production Functions*. Princeton: Princeton University Press.

Sherman, H.D. and Gold, F. 1985. "Bank Branch Operating Efficiency." *Journal of Banking and Finance* 9: 297-315.

Sheshinski, E. 1967. "Tests of 'Learning by Doing' Hypothesis." *Review of Economics and Statistics* 49: 569-578.

Silberberg, Eugene. *The Structure of Economics: A Mathematical Analysis*. New York: McGraw-Hill Book Company.

Sinkey, J.F., Jr. 1983. *Commercial Bank Financial Management*. New York: Macmillan Publishing Company.

Solow, R.M. 1957. "Technical Change and the Aggregate Production Function." *Review of Economics and Statistics* 39: 312-332.

--. 1965. "The Production Function and the Theory of Capital." *The Review of Economics and Statistics* 47: 101-108.

Srinivasan, A. 1992. "Are There Cost Savings From Bank Mergers?" *Economic Review* 77: 17-28. Atlanta: Federal Reserve Bank of Atlanta.

Stackelberg, H. von, 1952. *The Theory of the Market Economy.* Translated by A. T. Peacock. New York: Oxford University Press.

Stanback, T.M. and Noyelle, T.J. 1982. *Cities in Transition.* Totowa, New Jersey: Allanheld, Osmun & Co.

Stigler, G. 1987. *The Theory of Price.* New York: Macmilllan.

Taaffe, E.J, and Gauthier, H.L. 1973. *Geography of Transportation.* Englewood, NJ: Prentice-Hall, Inc.

Taylor, J.E. 1990. *The Process of Change in American Banking.* New York: Quorum Books.

Theil, H. 1978. *Introduction to Econometrics.* Englewood Cliffs, New Jersey: Prentice-Hall, Inc.

Thill, J.C. 1992. "Competitive Strategies for Multi-establishment Firms." *Economic Geography* 68: 290-308.

Thünen, J. H. von, 1826, *Der Isolierte Saat in Beziehung auf Landwirtschaft und Nationalekonomie.* Hamburg.

Tinbergen, J. 1962. *Shaping the World Economy: Suggestions for An International Economic Policy.* New York: Twentieth Century Fund.

Törnqvist, L. 1936. "The Bank of Finland's Consumption Index. *Bank of Finland Monthly Bulletin* 10: 1-8.

Wallis, Kenneth F. 1980. *Topics in Applied Econometrics.* Minneapolis: University of Minnesota Press.

Walras, L. 1954. *Elements of Pure Economics.* Translated by W. Jaffe. Homewood: Richard D. Irwin.

Watt, P.A. 1980. "Economies of Scale in Schools: Some Evidence From the Private Sector." *Applied Economics* 12: 235-242.

Weber, A. 1957. *Theory of Location of Industries.* Translated by C. J. Friedrich. Chicago: The University of Chicago Press.

Wheeler, J.O. and Dillon, P.M. 1985. "The Wealth of the Nation: Spatial Dimensions of U.S. Metropolitan Commercial Banking, 1970-1980." *Urban Geography* 6: 297-315.

Wheeler, J.O. 1986a. "The United States Metropolitan Corporate and Population Hierarchies, 1960-1980. *Geogrfiska Annales* 67: 89-97.

--. 1986b. "Corporate Spatial Links With Financial Institutions: the Role of the Metropolitan Hierarchy. *Annals of American Association of Geographers* 76: 262-274.

--. 1988. "Spatial Ownership Links of Major Corporation: Dallas and Pittsburgh Examples." *Economic Geography* 64: 1-16.

Wheeler, J.O. and Mitchelson, R.L. 1989. "Information Flows Among Major Metropolitan Areas in the United States." *Annals of the Association of American Geographers* 79: 524-543.

Wheeler, J.O. and Zhou, B. 1994. "Changes in Commercial Banking in the New U.S. Urban Service Economy, 1985-1990." *Abstracts, Association of American Geographers, 90th Annual Meeting*. Washington DC: Association of American Geographers.

White, L.H. 1993. Why is the U.S. Banking Industry in Trouble? In *The Crisis of American Banking*. L.H. White Ed. New York: the New York University Press.

Whitehead, D.D. 1983. *A Guide to Interstate Banking*. Atlanta: Federal Reserve Bank of Atlanta.

William A. and Haslem, John A. 1975. "Productive Efficiency in Commercial Banking." *Journal of Money, Credit, and Banking*. 7: 317-330.

Williamson, O. 1975. *Markets and Hierarchies: Analysis and Antitrust Implications*. New York: The Press.

--. 1986. *Economic Organization*. Brighton: Wheatsheaf Books.

Wilson, A.G. 1971. "A Family of Spatial Interaction Models, and Associated Developments." *Environment and Planning A* 3: 1-32.

Worthington, P.R. 1993. "Recent Trends in Corporate Leverage." *Economic Perspectives* May/June: 24-31. Chicago: Federal Reserve Bank of Chicago.

Zellner, A. 1962. "An Efficient Method of Estimating Seemingly Unrelated Regression Equations and Tests for Aggregation Bias." *Journal of the American Statistical Association* 57: 348-368.

Index

Accounting Procedure, 28, 164
Accounts, 169-170
Alonso-Muth Framework, 22
Assessment of Banking
  Performance, 7, 10, 27-32,
  169-187, 192-193
  See also Efficiency
Bank Holding Companies, 6,
  10, 15, 111-156,
  BankAmerica Corp., 147-
  153
  Bank of Boston, 147-150
  Chase Manhattan Corp.,
  147-153
  Citicorp, 147-148
  First Bank System, Inc.,
  147-148
  First Chicago Corp., 147-
  151
  First Interstate Bancorp,
  147-153
  First Union Corp., 147-153
  Harris Bankcorp, Inc., 147-
  151
  Keycorp, 147-153
  Fleet Financial Group, Inc.,
  147-153
  NationsBank, 147-153
  Norwest Holding Co., 147-
  149

  Shawmut National Corp.,
  147-153
  State Street Boston Corp.,
  147-153
  Wells Fargo & Company,
  147-152

Banking
  Branch, 14-15, 98-110
  Chain, 15
  Group, 15
  In-state, 15
  Interstate, 6-7, 15-19, 118-
  127, 191
  Intrastate, 112-117
  Multi-location, 5-7
Banking Assets, 5, 145-149,
  169-170
Banking Industry, 3-6
  Banking Crisis, 14
  Banking Deregulation, 5-6
  13
  Dual Banking System, 11
  History of U.S., 11-20
  Free Banking Movement 11-
  12
  Banking Reform, 5, 12-14
Banking Laws, 14-19
  Alabama, 15, 17-18
  Alaska, 15, 17-18
  Arizona, 15, 17-18